GOD

HELP ME
THROUGH
TODAY

GOD
HELP ME THROUGH TODAY

Psalm 23 Revisited

BOB LIVELY

MOREHOUSE PUBLISHING

Harrisburg, Pennsylvania

Morehouse Publishing
P.O. Box 1321
Harrisburg, PA 17015

Morehouse Publishing is a division of The Morehouse Group.

Cover design by Thomas Castanzo.

Library of Congress Cataloging-in-Publication Data

Lively, Robert Donald.
    God help me through today : Psalm 23 revisited / Bob Lively.
        p. cm.
    ISBN 0-8192-1871-5
    1. BIBLE. O.T. Psalms XXIII—Commentaries.   2. Fear—
Religious aspects—Christianity.   3. Christian life—Presbyterian
authors.   I. Title.
    BS1450 23rd.L58   2001
    242'.5—dc21   00-050068

Printed in the United States of America
01 02 03 04 05 06 07 08 09   10 9 8 7 6 5 4 3 2 1

*To Susan Ellen Wills
and Karen Adams Cox,
whose devotion to
abused children inspired this book*

Contents

Foreword

This small volume is the first book I know about that presents, for contemporary men and women, an honest and clear description of the classical "way of holiness." It is the most reality-oriented work on the meaning of the Twenty-third Psalm I have read.

This study is an extremely practical guide to spiritual and emotional recovery from fear. The healing comes through the transformation of pain and anxiety generated by our materialistic culture. Spiritual pilgrims of all kinds can find their way through these pages.

Coming out of the rich soil of his own theological and psychological education, Bob brings forth new wisdom about us and about the path toward God and freedom. He thoughtfully takes us through a labyrinth of our own pain and fear, as we follow him in his longing for and running from the love and guidance of the Good Shepherd. I certainly saw some of my own unspoken lifelong spiritual journey in these pages: the frantic yearning for success and recognition as a young man, the shock of failure and rejection, and finally the coming out of denial about my own dishonesty (with myself and people close to me). He shows us the agonizing terror and joy of finally turning loose, surrendering to God, and stepping across the threshold out of the prison of fear.

This book is filled with remarkable and surprising wisdom about spiritual leadership as well as guidance, all illustrated with stories from the life of a Texas sharecropper's son who has become one of the most authentic and committed spiritual guides I know anywhere.

It is my privilege to introduce to you a book that comes from a sensitive and refined intellect, made accessible and engaging by the vulnerable healing process the author describes.

J. KEITH MILLER
AUSTIN, TEXAS

Preface

I first heard Psalm 23 read aloud to me in 1950 by Mrs. Neeley, my beloved teacher during that very formative kindergarten year at the Oak Cliff Presbyterian Church Day School. I was four years old at the time, and though I had managed to learn to read a scattering of prepositions and adjectives, the eloquence and profundity of this masterpiece were far beyond the grasp of my mind. At the time I was occupied with making some kind of *literal* sense out of the myriad of wonders that comprised my small world.

Our beloved Mrs. Neeley read the words of this psalm to us several times during that year. I listened intently, though I no more knew what a shepherd was than I comprehended calculus. My granddaddy was a dairy man and a truck farmer in the Piney Woods of deep East Texas. Therefore, what little I had experienced in my initial four years of life in the context of animal husbandry had to do with cows, calves (I had not yet figured out the bull's role), chickens, pullets, pigs, and cur dogs. If there was at the midpoint of the twentieth century so much as one ram residing in Houston County, Texas, I was not aware of its existence.

The meaning of the words of this psalm remained abstract and its compelling imagery was all but lost on my very concrete perceptual frame of reality during those early years. To me the Psalm 23 was little more than a string of long, boring words which our teacher seemed to enjoy wasting my time reading in a stern tone that caused me to wonder if I was not about to be reprimanded for I could not imagine what.

I more or less ignored the psalmist's words as I meandered from childhood to adolescence because I was far too busy having fun to be much interested in anything religious. During those years both Sunday school and worship were nothing more to me than two hours I was required to endure weekly by parental edict.

If I thought of it at all, I attributed little significance to the psalm during those somewhat halcyon days comprising my four years of college. In short order I slipped from a sophomoric faith into an even more immature, not to mention amorphous and half-baked, agnosticism.

It was not until exactly twenty years after Mrs. Neeley first read these verses to me in kindergarten that I revisited them as a twenty-five-year-old intern pastor in the First Presbyterian Church of Fulton, Missouri. How could I ever forget that bitterly cold Missouri day? The temperature was prophesied by the weather sages in St. Louis and Kansas City not to climb above zero. Both radio stations further warned of an impending blizzard that was destined to hammer the Missouri-Iowa border before the faint glow of January sun had faded behind the stark winter horizon.

The night before this brutal dawn, I had visited an old man in the hospital who was suffering, unbeknownst to me, from the final stages of emphysema. What pastoral care training I had acquired could have been contained in a thimble, with plenty of room left over for my grandmother's finger. The old man, balanced on the edge of the hospital bed, gasping for breath with an oxygen tube in both nostrils, managed to whisper to me this unsettling question: "Bob, am I going to die?"

I dodged—I thought, artfully—his obvious expression of anxiety with the following insensitive response: "We're all going to die." I was not prepared for what followed, and his tone unnerved me. "But I mean tonight, son. Am I going to meet my Maker tonight?" Very gently I touched his shoulder so as to reassure him with what I concluded erroneously to be an absolute certainty. "No, you are not going to die tonight," I whispered in his ear as he continued to gasp for breath. "Why do not you lie back down now and get some rest? Tomorrow will come soon enough, but for tonight you can rest assured that you will wake up refreshed and surely more hopeful." In effect, in that awkward moment, I practiced medicine without a license because I offered this man a prognosis I had no right whatsoever to posit. Today I would know to treat the situation much differently.

The old man gratefully accepted my prognosis and reclined his head against the firm hospital pillow. He blinked several times before sleep came to assuage his worry. I watched gratefully, even feeling a touch of pride as the old man's breathing moved from tortured to still hollow, but more rhythmic. Slipping out of his room quietly, I half whispered to myself, "Good work, Lively. If only my seminary professors could see me now."

I was startled out of my sleep at five the next morning by the piercing ring of the wall phone in the hall. At first I incorporated the ring into my dream, but the phone's urgency refused to join me in becoming a symbol in the murky world of my unconscious mind. I staggered down the hallway to the phone, lifted the vibrating receiver from its steel cradle, and mumbled a feeble "Hello."

The church's pastor, a saint of a man who for the past year had served as my supervisor, was calling to inform me that the gentleman I had promised only hours before that he would not die, had, in fact, succumbed. Although it was cold enough in that hallway for me to see my breath, I sweat bullets as I heard the pastor tell me that the old man would be buried days later in the village of Bellflower, Missouri, not a stone's throw from the Iowa state line.

Then the pastor requested that I arrange my schedule to transport the man's widow to the funeral home in Bellflower that very morning. My reflexive reaction was to balk and then to make up some excuse why I could not drive that icy highway almost all the way to Iowa. I paused as I thought better of lying to a man for whom truth was the foundation of every decision. Counter to my selfishness, I feigned enthusiasm as I muttered a monosyllabic "yes" into the telephone's receiver.

Within two hours I was on the road to Bellflower, Missouri, with two passengers in tow—the widow of the man I had assured that he would live through the night and the man's sister. The latter half of that duo reclined on the back seat of my compact Chevrolet as she recited over and over again, seemingly ad infinitum and for me precariously close to ad nauseam, Psalm 23. As I glanced in the rearview mirror in time to see the Fulton, Missouri city limits sign, I recall her mumbling the words, "Yea, though I walk through the valley of the shadow." As I stopped to fill up my nearly empty gas tank, shivering on that numbingly cold morning, I watched in bewilderment and annoyance as the deceased man's sister fogged the car's back window by continuing to recite the words of that psalm.

Today I recognize that for her this rote recitation was a comforting, though seemingly compulsive, defense against the terrifying thoughts I could only imagine were at that moment swirling about in her mind. But in those anxious hours the woman's incessant recitation of the song grated on my nerves with a discordance similar to a carpenter foolishly planing against the grain. My being began to vibrate with anger that tangled up with my apprehension regarding the coming blizzard. Still the woman went on reciting the words. Over and over again she said them. Every time she arrived at the psalm's comforting conclusion, I would hold my breath and silently beseech the God I believed capable of parting the Red Sea to put an immediate halt to this old woman's pious prattling.

My selfish prayer proved ineffectual, so I turned my thoughts to beseeching the Almighty to hold off on the blizzard until such time as I might get myself and two old women out of northern Missouri and return the three of us safely to our homes and hearths in Fulton. To my delight, this second prayer seemed to work, or at the very least the forces that cause blizzards elected to wait until the man's widow completed the necessary arrangements with the funeral director. Meanwhile, her sister-in-law rattled on about green pastures and still waters.

As we turned the Chevrolet's balding front tires toward home, jumbo snow flakes pelted the windshield. After more than a few hazardous slips and angular slides on that Missouri highway, we gratefully rolled into the seat of Calloway County, Missouri, a town that for one interesting year I called home. Throughout the whole of that frightening drive, the woman in the back seat never ceased her recitation. She offered not so much as one word of social amenity.

If familiarity does, indeed, breed contempt, I must confess to having held this psalm in mild contempt since that cold day in Missouri. In the last few years, however, I have discovered that its simple beauty points to a depth that awes. As I was preparing a lecture one day in the early '90s, I again happened upon the words I had intentionally avoided ever since that inhospitable mid-western winter day long ago. After reading them carefully with the perspective afforded by some small measure of maturity, I experienced a sudden exhilaration most every human being, or, at least the fortunate among us, experiences when unexpectedly uncovering a treasure.

As I read the words this time, I could no longer hear the woman's grating prattle ringing in my ears. Gratefully, I read the words of Psalm 23 a second time and then a third, and each time I read them, I saw something in them that I had never discovered before. Much to my amazement, I believe I bumped into God's treatment plan for our fear and anxiety—contained in a mere 113 words. Consequently, what I offer in this brief book is not so much an exposition of Psalm 23 as it is the fleshing out of what I discern to be a sound strategy for turning a life of fear into an existence where joy is palpable and serenity is the norm.

Not long ago I was walking in the Texas hill country, which is my daily habit, and I heard my own voice whisper a seemingly bizarre message to me amidst the daily confusion that blows through my mind. It was this: "You are to help children." At first, of course, I possessed no clear idea what these words meant, but I listened and I paid attention. For months prior to hearing that message, I had been asking God to grant me the clarity I yearned for so that I might know what God would have me do next with my life. In the wake of that prayer came the unsettling words: "You are to help children."

Except for a brief season as a kindergarten teacher, I never really worked much with children. In the early part of my pastoral career I assisted others in forming several nonprofit corporations that served the needs of the homeless and desperate of Dallas, but seldom in those years did I work specifically with children. I helped found a day camp and a self-esteem program for children from poor families in south Dallas, but I always hired professionals who were trained in early childhood development to do the actual hands-on work with the little ones.

Consequently, I was bewildered by what I heard those words advising me to do. By the end of the walk, however, the bewilderment turned to a clarity that seems as rare in my mind as a downpour in a Texas drought. I arrived home, fed my two cats, picked up the kitchen telephone, and called my friend Susan Wills, executive director of the Austin Children's Shelter. When she answered the phone, I announced to her that I was called to write a book, to somehow get it published, and to donate 50 percent of the proceeds to the agency she serves, the Austin Children's Shelter, and the other 50 percent to Court Appointed Special Advocates of Travis County, or CASA. Susan was thrilled with the news, and I hung up the phone wondering what it was that I had just promised to do.

What you hold in your hands is a response to the inner voice I heard advising me in a solemn whisper to help abused and neglected children. I am convinced the voice told me to write about Psalm 23 because a Power far greater than I wanted me to discover among other things, that this psalm is, indeed, God's way of helping us through each day.

Today I am bold enough to believe that I have lived long enough and have visited the valley of the shadow of death and supped at the table prepared for me before my enemies with sufficient frequency to have some insights to offer others. In this book I will share heaven's treatment plan for what I believe ails every human being—fear. Two decades ago I only knew to run from these words. Today it is my hope and my sincere prayer that through Psalm 23 the reader will experience God's love helping him or her through each day. If something I write here does, in fact, prove helpful to the reader, to him who inspired this poem three millennia ago goes the glory. May the words that follow bring hope to those little ones who have been abandoned, neglected, or abused.

Acknowledgments

This book came into being through the inspiration of God shining through the lives of the men and women who form the community I know as "the church" here in Austin, Texas. Any list I compile will, no doubt, omit the names of people who should be included. What follows is only a partial record of those who have contributed to the writing of *God Help Me Through Today*. First a word of thanks to Linda and Michael Byrd who so generously published the first version of this book to help abused children. I give thanks to Dr. Robert Moats and Dr. Greg Maksymowicz for caring for me as I walked "the valley." Thanks to Karen Cox and Susan Wills who applauded from the beginning the writing of this book. My appreciation to the volunteers who gave so generously of their time and talent, including editor Chris Liechti and proofreaders Mary Louise McKaughan, Marilyn Galloway, and Trish Bell. I am also grateful to Dr. Robert M. Shelton, President of Austin Presbyterian Theological Seminary, Edith Royal, and Laura Bush, the First Lady of Texas, for their willingness to join me in raising a community's consciousness regarding the welfare of children.

My trusted and gifted colleague Elaine Galloway deserves as much credit for this book as do I. Her encouragement nurtured me on a daily basis. I offer heartfelt thanks also to Alice Travis for her enthusiasm, which served to convince me that the first draft of this book was worthy of development.

To my family, my wife Mary Lynn, my precious daughter Sarah, and my parents and brothers who have loved me since the beginning, thank you for praying for me as I wrote. To my mentor J. Keith Miller, who so generously provided the foreword for this work and whose book *The Taste of New Wine* launched me on this journey, I proclaim a loud and hearty "thank you!" for his willingness to love me into believing in myself.

I thank Kathleen Niendorff who has to be the most conscientious and knowledgeable literary agent in the world. The professional commitment she demonstrates is rare and inspiring. Also, I thank Dr. Mark Fretz of Morehouse Publishing Group for his many excellent editorial suggestions.

To the one who made me and whose rod and staff comforted me every step of the way as I wrote, I pray that the words I have written will touch lives for his name's sake and help children who have been wounded beyond what most of us can imagine.

Introduction

On an unseasonably warm autumn afternoon I rested my aching back against an adobe wall that my Native American guide informed me had been constructed in the thirteenth century. For the sake of convenience, this guide's Acoma name had been distilled down to the two Anglicized syllables "Su-zie." Her name is not likely to stump the horde of tourists who regularly toss a half dollar in her direction in exchange for a photo of her posing with their children born, reared, and insulated from the ravages of economic deprivation in affluent suburbs of the United States.

The tour she had offered me was finished. For the past hour we had strolled about the dusty, winding paths of a tiny adobe village that was spread out like a rumpled tablecloth on the low summit of a mesa in western New Mexico. As the afternoon sun dipped below the dramatic horizon in a land that fully lives up to its billing as the habitation of enchantment, Suzie and I waited on a bench in awkward silence for a school bus to transport us from the village to the visitor center five hundred feet below.

The fading streaks of the October afternoon etched a silent benediction across the orange sky, and I watched in fascination as an Acoma shepherd herded his flock from a distant meadow toward a stone fold where they might be protected for the night from whatever predators roamed the valley below. Their formation intrigued me as much as did the rhythmic, circular flow of their movement. It was as though a cloud far beneath me was billowing on the valley floor. The energy that formed its.essence seemed to flow from the center to the outer boundaries of this huge circle consisting of several hundred sheep. Curiously, the circle never lost its shape as it "floated" westward toward the stone fold.

Upon closer examination, I discovered in the growing shadows of the afternoon that a single shepherd trailed behind the flock while two well-trained sheep dogs on the perimeter kept the sheep moving in a westward direction while maintaining the distinctly circular formation.

Immediately, I thought of Isaiah's penetrating insight into the core of human nature expressed in the following indictment: "All we like sheep have gone astray; we have turned every one to his own way . . ." (Isa. 53:6). It was obvious that without the shepherd behind them to point them toward the fold and the ever-vigilant dogs to keep the animals in formation, every one of those wayward creatures would have wandered aimlessly no doubt to their own detriment if not to death about the valley below.

The shepherd reminded me of my earliest years, when my granddaddy would grant me permission to walk to the pasture in search of his herd of cows. To this day I am not sure why his signal for permission brought me such joy. Probably I enjoyed the brief illusion of possessing some power in a world where any real power and authority seemed as far removed from my experience as flying is from an Angus bull. For maybe as long as one-half hour each evening I was in charge of those huge animals, and I roared at them all manner of marching orders to which they paid no attention as they ponderously lumbered toward the milking pen.

I recalled those seemingly glorious moments of nothing more substantive than feigned power as I watched the shepherd and his dogs work those sheep until they delivered them to a safe place in a wilderness probably as pristine and wild as one can find today.

In that moment of tired reflection I concluded that sheep are not terribly bright. Until that moment and based upon my experience of driving cows to the milking pen, I would have sworn to anyone and wagered as much as a whole box of Crackerjacks to all comers that the bovine mind just had to be *the* most limited of all farm animals. But compared to the behavior I witnessed that October afternoon, I decided every cow I had ever met, driven, or fed was deserving of an honorary doctorate compared to those sheep. Without the shepherd and his dedicated dogs, those animals would have been hopelessly lost and at more risk than I was up to imagining in the chill of the coming evening.

The school bus finally arrived and transported me and my guide "Suzie" to the visitor center below where I tipped her a buck or so and bade her farewell. Driving toward the room I had rented for my night's lodging, I summoned the courage to reflect upon the ancient poet's now, to me, amazingly fitting image of God as the shepherd and of us human beings as wayward sheep. We also are hopelessly lost without guidance from beyond the boundaries of both our individual and collective selves. Only in the last few years have I returned to Psalm 23 as a source of comfort and wisdom. Now, every time I read the opening five words, "The Lord is my shepherd," I am immediately transported in my mind back to the summit of that mesa in New Mexico with the teeming flock of sheep and the caring shepherd below.

Having sojourned with this song long enough to probe its depths, I further concluded that this one poem, consisting of only six verses, teaches us everything we need to know about life. It tells us who God is—the shepherd. It informs us who we are—sheep. It whispers rather than trumpets the shape human existence inevitably assumes—a journey. It imparts to us what we can expect to rely on as guides along the way—the shepherd's rod and staff. It warns us where our travel will invariably take us—into the valley of the shadow of death. It points out who we will encounter along the way—enemies. It also offers us something amazing that sheep could never dream of. It assures us in nothing less than the imagery reserved for royalty what will be the eventual outcome of that taxing encounter—an anointing. Finally, it proclaims our ultimate destiny—the "house of the Lord for ever."

Every reading of Psalm 23 evokes a response and what follows in this book is mine. I do not believe that poetry can ever be explained. Perhaps it cannot even be interpreted. I do know that thirty years ago I sat through one poetry and literature class after another in pursuit of a minor in English. During those days of undergraduate study, I met several course requirements by what were evaluated as more-than-satisfactory "explications" of poetry. Today, however, with sufficient life experience in my rearview mirror to qualify me as seasoned, I have come to believe that poetry, especially that which we hold to be divinely inspired, proclaims its own unique truth to the subjective mind and soul of the reader, without the need of interpretation by someone else, even a respected biblical scholar, which I am not.

The songs we find in the Bible, especially the psalms, are the passionate expression of some ancient soul's transformative encounter with divine mystery. Therefore, each song offers a timeless word that mystery bequeaths to the ages and that has its origin in a divine inspiration beyond the comprehension of even the poet. Each encounter with the song is its own unique and, if read reverently and prayerfully, hallowed experience.

When we pause to read and ponder these songs, our minds are intersecting with far more than the residue of that ancient encounter of mystery with soulful artistry. If we view them only as relics of the distant past, we might regard them as no more alive than some 50-year-old snapshot gathering dust in our grandmother's photo album. The reality in any experience with biblical poetry is that our encounter is not only with the song, but also invariably with the source of that song who is ultimate mystery and the one Jesus called Father.

Psalm 23 is not some rusted-out relic frozen in time. Rather this poem is an active organism whose source is alive and can inspire today's spiritual traveler with soul-penetrating truth every bit as much as it fired the passion of the one who first scratched its magnificence upon ancient papyrus. Consequently, for one to be presumptuous enough to believe that he or she can interpret, much less explain, that which is dynamic as opposed to static, is akin to marking the presence of a cloud on a high mountain peak. The cloud might hover above the peak for as long as a week. In a scientific and metaphorical sense, the cloud would possess its own identity and its identity would be unique. Although it might resemble other phenomena with its form and composition correlating with standard meteorological taxonomy, it would still be the expression of forces that were unique to that moment in time.

A person would be foolish to attempt to scale a tall peak in the cause of marking the cloud. By the time he or she arrived at the summit, the cloud would likely have disappeared or, at the very least, have changed itself into another shape or joined with the forces of nature to become a very different kind of cloud.

The cloud as an analogy breaks down here—fails to hold water—when compared to the eternal quality of God's word. Be that as it may, I submit that like the cloud, the songs of God may only be experienced in much the same way as the wind in our hair, or the summer rain washing against our face, or the birth cry of an infant, or mud squeezing between our toes, or the fragrance of a tomato shoot, or a dove's coo, or that last gulp of homemade fudge marble ice cream.

These songs are alive only because their inspiration lives. I have come to believe that they are given to us as a gift. By virtue of the fact that God has created us as individuals, we have the unmerited opportunity to experience life, including its fear, suffering, and bewilderment. The psalms are a gift to us because through them we may come to know what it means to trust the inspiration behind the poetry—the psalmist's shepherd, the one whom Jesus called Father.

This book is the expression of what I learned from God's song at a time in my life when circumstances beyond the boundaries of my control have compelled me to trust mystery. I have never been much inclined to trust anyone but myself or anything but my own conclusions and subsequent solutions. However, at this time in my life, when middle age has collided with heart-ache, I have finally come to understand what wiser people have discovered much earlier in life—trusting in the Good Shepherd is the only sane way for me to live.

As I pondered and lived these words for months, I believe I discovered that what this psalm represents to me in these middle years of life is what I might best describe as a "treatment plan" for fear and anxiety. If I were to have written this book ten years ago or if I were to write it ten years from now, it might mean something entirely different to me. Psalm 23 is not exclusively a treatment plan for fear and anxiety, but perhaps it is because I stand in need of such a plan that I discern one in it.

As always when I write, my prayer is this: "God, please help someone who is hurting badly to realize through my words that you are love, and not shame, and that it is by your grace, and only by your grace, that any of us is ever really healed, and thank you for Psalm 23 as your help through our days."

Psalm 23

The Lord is my shepherd; I shall not want.
He maketh me to lie down in green pastures:
he leadeth me beside the still waters.

He restoreth my soul: he leadeth me in the paths
of righteousness for his name's sake.

Yea, though I walk through the valley of the shadow of death,
I will fear no evil: for thou art with me;
thy rod and thy staff they comfort me.

Thou preparest a table before me
in the presence of mine enemies:
thou anointest my head with oil;
my cup runneth over.

Surely goodness and mercy shall follow me
all the days of my life:
and I will dwell in the house of the Lord for ever.

Authorized King James Version

The Lord is My Shepherd

P salm 23 opens with a simple affirmation. "The Lord is my shepherd" articulates a profound truth in only five words. Next to the proclamation that Christ is Lord, these five words may be the most profound realization ever to flow from the human mind and into written expression. What the poet states is the only true perspective that a human being can have if he or she ever hopes to discover complete healing.

From the very beginning, our culture lies to us. It even conspires with biology to play a trick on us. The consequence of this trick is that it deceives us into believing that we are the center of the universe. Why should we not believe this? After all, every time we as infants so much as whimper or whine, someone pops a flesh or plastic nipple into our gaping mouth. We are nourished while we learn to embrace the insidious message that we are the center of everything. Consequently, we come to believe that all we must do to get what we want is raise a ruckus and, in functional families at least, our every legitimate need is met immediately.

Though this kind of conditioning continues throughout childhood and sometimes well into young adult life, along the way we are also socialized to assume appropriate responsibility for ourselves and for our every decision. This is a necessary lesson that every human being must learn if he or she is to function with any hope of real success in life. The hidden side of this message, however, can slip into blatant heresy. If it does, it turns into a mistaken idea: Because I must learn to assume responsibility for myself and my decisions and my triumphs as well as my disappointments, I am, therefore, wholly responsible for this life, totally in charge of myself and everything about me. I am, therefore, the captain of my own ship and the master of my fate.

There are many in the secular world of that soft science known as psychology, as well as in other fields, including religion, who would argue vehemently that the above statement is not heresy, but is rather a harsh existential reality that must be embraced by every individual. I disagree with that theory and, obviously, so does the ancient poet who three thousand years ago offered to the ages these amazing five words:

The Lord is my shepherd . . .

Here is a truth that cannot fully be appreciated by so-called successful people who have yet to experience real failure or tragedy. They, like me during the first four decades of my life, fairly well under the illusion that because they have worked hard and have made a string of good and, in the main, ethical decisions, they are successful according to this world's standards. They likely married well and today they live in a desirable part of town where the schools are good. They belong to churches and synagogues filled with nice people who, not unlike themselves, are affluent and very respectable. They pay their taxes on time; vacation annually in fun, if not exotic, locales; and some hold memberships in all the right clubs.

Life seems to work splendidly for them. More in line with their illusion, they have, they believe, learned to work life. So one day in Sunday school or Hebrew school or worship, they hear a teacher, pastor, or rabbi read these astounding words, "The Lord is my shepherd," and the penetrating profundity of their meaning bounces off their illusion of self-sovereignty like rain drumming its steady cadence against a tin roof.

Sadly, perhaps even ironically, it requires tragedy, the kind that rattles one's convictions so thoroughly that one is forced to question everything about life, for these words to mean what the poet intended. As I read this poem, it is apparent to me that these ancient words were written in the wake of some personal disaster.

Imagine, if you will, King David, the greatest king Israel was ever to produce, as the author of these amazing five words. Here is a man who was a living legend even before he was old enough to shave. Standing alone before the most feared warrior of his day, he reached into his pouch and removed one of five smooth stones. Placing it in his sling, he slew a giant of a man named Goliath with nothing more than the skill he had learned as a shepherd boy. From this moment on, he lived a rags-to-riches existence as the greatest figure since Moses, as well as the very prototype, in the collective imagination of his people, of the form the messiah, the anointed one of Israel, would assume.

Not for three centuries had there been and not for a thousand more years would there be one so magnificent and so celebrated, yet David is credited with writing "The Lord is my shepherd." What can this possibly mean? In my mind it can translate into only one thing: His illusion of being the captain of his ship or the master of his fate had gone awry. We know from the biblical testimony that such is true. His adulterous relationship with the beautiful Bathsheba eventuated in his decision to arrange the death, in reality to murder, her husband Uriah.

At first David seemed to get away with this scheme, although in 2 Samuel we read "...the thing that David had done displeased the Lord" (11:27). Consequently, the Lord sent Nathan the prophet to David to prick his conscience to the point of bringing him to full awareness regarding the heinous sin he had committed. As is the case with all of us, it was easier for this mighty king of Israel to hear a veiled metaphor concealing the content of his sin than it would ever have been for him to accept from a lowly prophet a head-on collision with the truth.

Nathan cleverly captured the king's attention as he crafted a tale of two men, both of whom owned sheep. The first man in Nathan's story was characterized as rich in that he possessed many herds and flocks. But the other protagonist was so poor that he had nothing more to show for a lifetime of labor than one little ewe.

Every good story necessarily contains three essential elements: (1) colorful characters, (2) a plot, and (3) trouble. Nathan's story possessed all three. Once David had been introduced to the rich man and the poor man in this story, Nathan developed the plot involving a sojourner who arrives in the home of the rich man. Once a plot is established in any good story, trouble can never be far behind.

Nathan, the storyteller, did not disappoint his king. He continued this tale by telling David that the rich man, who was very selfish, takes the poor man's little ewe and slaughters it and prepares a meal for his house guest.

David was outraged at such odious injustice. The king railed at the prophet Nathan, "As the Lord lives, the man who has done this deserves to die; and he shall restore the lamb fourfold, because he did this thing, and because he had no pity" (2 Sam. 12:6).

Nathan now had David exactly where he wanted him. Though Scripture does not record it, in my mind's eye I can hear the prophet stringing the king along with a dramatic and pregnant pause as he permits this powerful, and now enraged, man to catch his breath. I suspect that it was with what just had to be perfect timing and with perhaps a knowing glance offered over his shoulder as he turned to walk away—Nathan whispered to the king this devastating charge: "You are the man" (2 Sam. 12:7).

If David is, in fact, the writer of Psalm 23, imagine the shift that occurred in him from seemingly boundless hubris to a now-immortal expression of humility. For the second word of the poem almost screams humility; of course, that word is "Lord." It is clear from the start that someone else, and not the author, is the lord of his or her life.

Since Abraham Lincoln's Emancipation Proclamation, all of us in this country have enjoyed a legacy of liberty bequeathed to us by those who came before, so we may find it impossible to appreciate the full impact of the connotations inherent in that one word, "Lord." But in "Lord" we have the fullest possible expression of the sovereignty of God in the life of the poet. This word tells us that the writer obviously does not regard himself or herself as the master of his or her own existence. Rather, the poet has become convinced that the one Israel knew as Lord was fully in charge and in control of his or her life.

What it meant to be the subject of an earthly lord in ancient society may best be described in this one word—subjugation. One who was subjugated to the authority of another possessed absolutely no rights. Consequently, all rights were determined by the one they called "Lord." This arrangement penetrated every layer of the relationship shared between the Lord and his subject. Simply put, the relationship involved absolute acquiescence.

In our democratic society, thank God, no relationships exist that even remotely resemble the power intended when the poet declares that mighty word "Lord." We may at first think of landlords, but such an image is not even in the same ballpark with what is symbolized in the ancient relationship between a lord and his subject. In the early years of my adult life I changed residences, therefore landlords, every year or so. As best I can recall, I paid them by mail each month and hardly ever saw them unless the plumbing broke or the air-conditioning ceased to function on a miserably hot Texas summer afternoon. Today I do not even recall their names. Obviously they possessed little real power in my life.

The word "boss" also doesn't really begin to approach the full impact the poet intends. A boss or supervisor is someone to whom we must adapt, even if we believe that he or she might be less than competent. If we hope to keep our jobs, we must necessarily conform to their expectations and to some extent please them with our performance; but there is a world of difference between compliance with expectations and total surrender. A boss or supervisor is only in charge of evaluating our work performance and has no say whatsoever in the myriad issues that comprise our personal lives.

For one brief stint of five years, I was a boss myself. Like most people, I have also experienced twenty-five years of supervisors. Through it all, some of those men and women were both competent and dedicated. Others were folks I merely endured while I did what I felt called to do, trying for the most part to stay out of their way so as not to threaten further their obvious (to me) insecurities. I suspect most who read this book may have had similar experiences.

This Lord is the one to whom the poet pays homage. The writer lives in awe of one far more powerful than any human being. For awe is what the word "Lord" first suggests, and the awe expressed here outstrips even the deepest meaning of the word respect. When the poet writes "Lord," this is the bold, but amazingly humble, recognition that someone else is in charge of his or her entire life—which means, of course, his or her every thought, decision, and act. This one word is a profound but surprisingly simple expression of what surrender invariably requires. The writer is proclaiming here, without even so much as a hint of equivocation, that his or her existence and every detail associated with it, including personal possessions and real estate, belong wholly to someone else.

Subservience is a radical position for anyone to assume, but this, nevertheless, is precisely the perspective of the poet. The writer is declaring with the first word past the definite article "The" that his or her life is totally surrendered, or in submission, to one called "Lord."

The descriptive word provided to amplify this challenging declaration is every bit as intriguing as the pronouncement is daring. The poem tells us that this lord is simply a shepherd. Therefore, this lord is neither some tyrant nor a coercive dictator, but rather he is one who directs his sheep and saves them from their stupidity.

As mentioned in the Introduction, compared to a sheep, every cow I ever herded possessed the native intelligence necessary to become a candidate for a doctoral degree. Consequently, herding cows is very different from shepherding lambs. Cows are bright enough to require coercion. During the branding season their decisions must be redirected by a cowboy on a well-trained cutting horse. To handle a calf, a lariat and a tie rope are required. In truth, being a cowboy is hard, backbreaking, hot, dirty work that doesn't even come close to resembling the romantic image portrayed on television and in the movies.

The handling of sheep is a much different experience. Sheep are never roped or coerced, and outside of Luke's Christmas story, have you ever thought of shepherds as romantic figures? There is no NFL team that employs shepherds as mascots. Cowboys are romantic enough to suffice as the mascot for "America's team," but any franchise that chose to call themselves "The Shepherds" would be laughed out of the league. As I know from watching the Native-American shepherd work his flock from my lonely place on the summit of that mesa in New Mexico, I would say that these wayward animals are best led by subtle suggestions, hints, signs, signals, and sometimes gentle nudges.

When I think of cowboys, I dredge up flamboyant images of tough, swaggering, hard-drinking, fiercely independent men who were courageous enough to drive thousands of cattle out of Texas to the railheads in Kansas for nothing more than a pocket full of change. But when I hear the word "shepherd," a different image pops into my imagination. Immediately, I think of humility.

Shepherds are humble and at times courageous "drivers" who defend their sheep, suggest rather than coerce, hint and nudge rather than rope, throw down, force, pin, and brand. Consequently, with the introduction of the word "shepherd" into the poem, there appears a sudden and inevitable collision between the word "Lord," which suggests sovereignty, and the image of a shepherd, which with equal force signals humility. If this one to whom the poet has surrendered is, indeed, Lord, he must also be a humble sovereign in that he willingly assumes the role of a tender-but-brave shepherd.

To what do these apparently contradictory descriptive terms point? The term "shepherd" is the most descriptive word available to humanity in any language to describe the form, if not the process, of how God works. Employing a twentieth-century construct, I have come to believe that God resides in the unconscious of every human being to guide and direct us much like the shepherd I witnessed in New Mexico guided his flock—from behind and with the assistance of able sheepdogs.

"Behind" is an apt symbol for the unconscious. It seemed to me that the sheep below me in the valley never saw the shepherd, but their slow, steady movement in the direction of the stone fold convinced me that they knew and felt his abiding presence. There can be no question that he was the driving, but always unseen, force directing their individual and collective lives.

I suspect God seldom appeals to the conscious mind or to what the disciples of psychoanalytic theories term the ego. No, God seems far more frequently to work behind the scenes like the Acoma shepherd guiding individual sheep, as well as the flock as a whole, toward their destiny. Like the shepherd, God seems to signal us from behind with hints, suggestions, nudges, impulses, and unseen but powerful symbols. This is what I mean by God operating in the unconscious. Like a shepherd who stands behind us, God resides in the unconscious and visits, if you will. At times he even penetrates our defenses to show us the direction we are to go. Whether we are aware of it or not, God is always there and always in charge and always guiding us like an unobtrusive shepherd.

If we could interview a flock of sheep, we would, I am certain, hear them describe their shepherd as not only the lord of their flock, but also the lord of their individual destinies. They would further inform us that they seldom see this shepherd, but that his unseen presence is the most important reality in their lives. Without him, they would say unequivocally, they could not possibly find their way home to the fold. And without the safety of the fold, they likely would not survive the night. In a very real sense they would tell us that this shepherd is their "salvation," even though they seldom catch so much as a glimpse of him.

I do not think it is too much of a stretch for us to believe that Jesus was alluding to God as the shepherd on the "hidden side" or, using modern language, in the unconscious part of our lives, when he proclaimed the paradoxical notion of blessings being inherent in being poor. In Matthew's Gospel we hear him say, "Blessed are the poor in spirit, for theirs is the kingdom of heaven" (Matt. 5:3).

How else could there be a blessing in suffering unless the pain is to be regarded as a metaphorical shepherd guiding us to look where we have failed to search for truth? It instructs us to be grateful for the hurt we experience as we learn to view pain as a profound teacher. This is subtle stuff. In fact, it is so subtle as to be lost on most of us, but it was not lost on Jesus: he dared to proclaim from the top of a mountain that an enormous blessing is waiting to be discovered in our suffering, if only we are willing to plumb its depths.

What Jesus is saying is that it is our suffering that brings us to God. One of the miracles of the unconscious is that it brings to our conscious mind symbols that science terms "symptoms" that are the physical manifestations of our suffering. Sometimes those symbols (or symptoms) are quite severe, as in the case of a major depression, but far more often those symbols are hints and urges and bumps and nudges pointing us toward where we would not go if left to our own devices. What is amazing about those hints from the unconscious is that once they are heeded, they inevitably point us toward the truth that spiritual development requires we discover.

I doubt that we are ever really wise enough to differentiate between a shepherd's nudge emanating out of our unconscious and our more conscious perceptions of reality except when we gaze in the rearview mirror of our lives. But sometimes it happens that we see something and we decide, even against our better judgment and against all of our customary inhibitions, to take a huge risk.

When I was twenty-eight years old, I was traveling back to the Ozarks from my first semester of working on a doctorate at Austin Presbyterian Theological Seminary. At the time I was an instructor in religion and philosophy at a tiny liberal arts college in North Arkansas, and I decided to stop off in Dallas to visit with a search committee at the First Presbyterian Church that had expressed an interest in considering me for a position on its pastoral staff. Actually, my decision to stop in Dallas was fueled by nothing more than courtesy as opposed to any real interest in the position. Because I had been raised in Dallas, I had decided that it would be far wiser for me to grow professionally elsewhere.

On my way to the interview, I drove through the maze of corridors connecting downtown Dallas in search of a church I had only visited one time. It was during the driving rainstorm that imposed itself upon that otherwise uneventful Saturday morning that I saw God. While I do not ordinarily buy into literalism when it comes to interpreting the Scripture, I remain convinced that I did, indeed, see God. That is because I interpret literally the words of Jesus contained in Matthew's Gospel when he proclaims: "As you did it to one of the least of these my brethren, you did it to me" (Matt 25:40).

It was in that downpour that God quite unexpectedly showed up in the form of a bedraggled, rain-soaked beggar perched on the curb with what remained of his shoes submerged beneath the torrent of water flooding the street. As I paused at a stop light, I caught no more than a glimpse of his misery as he dug feverishly into a discarded box of fried chicken and gnawed like some starved dog on a half-eaten chicken bone.

A half hour later I was sitting before a committee of respectable Presbyterians who interviewed me for a position I had convinced myself I really didn't want. I entertained their rather anemic questions with equally disinterested responses, but deep inside I pondered the symbolic meaning of the man I had earlier witnessed gnawing on a drumstick in a rainstorm. Once they finished with their questions, the senior pastor leaned forward and said something that immediately appealed to my unhealthy grandiosity. He said, "You can go somewhere else and read church history or you can come here and make it."

Two weeks later I visited with my colleagues at the college in Arkansas and assured them that I had no intention of leaving. The very next morning as I relaxed in the rocking chair of my tiny office in the chapel studying the shadows playing their tricks on the blue foothills of the Ozark Mountains, I once more remembered that poor beggar in the rain. Much to my astonishment, I picked up the telephone, called the church in Dallas, and accepted the position.

Ten years later I left that church, but not after I had joined with literally countless saints in founding a soup kitchen, a free-standing all-night shelter for the homeless, a housing ministry for desperate families, a battered women's shelter, and various other ministries for the poor and the desperate of Dallas. It would prove to be the most remarkable ten years that I have yet lived, and I am convinced that the Good Shepherd simply showed up during that rainstorm and guided me back to my hometown where I was directed every frustrating step of the way in encouraging that church to incarnate Jesus' words regarding compassion toward those whom he called "the least of these."

For the vast majority of my life, God has remained behind me, in my unconscious, guiding me with symbols which in my subjective experience have most often manifested themselves through depression and anxiety. Every time I sink into a depression, which fortunately most often arrives in mild episodes, it means that I have ceased trusting God and once more have begun to scare myself into believing two terribly insidious lies that lead to one very unhealthy conclusion. The lies are these: (1) I am the sovereign of my life, (2) I am, therefore, responsible for everything. The conclusion is this: I must be perfect.

My pain then arrives as the unconscious shepherd who delivers me time and time again to the words of Jesus concerning the blessings inherent in those whose spirit is poor. Following this slow recognition of my spiritual error, I surrender my will again and again to God and, in time, venture into the place of trusting heaven with my life. Eventually, but seldom immediately, the fear and sadness lift and I step forward taking life one day at a time, quietly rejoicing. I then give thanks to a God who loves me so passionately that he is perfectly willing to reside mysteriously inside my unconscious, to provide me with the gift of pain whenever I make the error of convincing myself that I am sovereign.

Pain is all that possesses sufficient power to cause anyone to surrender in the manner in which the author of this poem has obviously submitted himself or herself to the authority of one who is called "my shepherd." We human beings do not simply decide to step out of the illusion of sovereignty on our own. Something must drive us from such an entrenched perspective. Pain, or that more protracted anguish we know as suffering, is all that is sufficiently powerful to push, shove, drive, or drag us kicking and screaming through our natural resistance to change and eventually, but seldom immediately, into the warm glow of healing.

I do not know of one surrendered man or woman who has not been through a personal dark night that might be described as "on earth as it is in hell." Moreover, I have yet to meet one spiritually mature human being who has not hit some kind of bottom. In fact, some of the most spiritually mature people I have encountered are those who are active in the Recovery Movement. Ironically, some of the most narcissistic, spiritually immature individuals I have ever encountered have been tall steeple preachers and leaders in the institutional church.

For those of us who have hit bottom, the first five words of this poem are laden with meaning because it is only through our suffering that we become convinced that God is God and we are his, not the other way around. Further, we have learned through experience—not by reading books and hearing sermons—that God's love is so pervasive that it greets us even in the form of pain, for the purpose of returning us to a place of healing.

I have hit bottom. The details of that experience may be expressed briefly. People I regarded as close friends and colleagues unexpectedly abandoned me professionally one cold February morning, and I was left standing alone in the courtyard of a church where I didn't know what else to do but to surrender everything to God. And that is exactly what I did.

As wrenching as that experience was, I have discovered that many people have experienced similar crises. (As I stated above, I have yet to meet a spiritually mature human being who has not experienced and endured pain.) They soon discovered that their suffering was the most efficacious teacher ever sent to bring them to their knees so that they might come to recognize that God is sovereign.

One such man is my friend Jerry. Fifteen years ago this man, who holds a Ph.D. in sociology, served on the faculty of the University of Texas. By his own admission he was an atheist, which in spiritual terms quite likely meant that he had at some level decided that he was the sovereign of his own existence. His wife Judy reported to him her mild surprise at being pregnant in midlife, and some months later she delivered an infant daughter born with Down's syndrome.

Initially Jerry was shocked, but this numbness soon enough turned to an anger that became tangled with bewilderment. Shortly after his daughter's birth he traveled to Washington, DC. on business. During a lull in his schedule, he happened into the National Cathedral one afternoon in time to hear the choir practicing its Sunday anthems. As the afternoon light streamed through the stained glass, Jerry became suddenly aware that a power he had never dared to confront before was now burning deeply inside him and searing his resolve to remain centered in himself.

To make the proverbial long story short, Jerry returned to Texas, left his position at the university, and converted to Catholicism. He and his wife and their daughter Kelly founded a ranch ministry east of Austin where they offer job training and a summer camp experience for mentally retarded adults and adolescents.

Today my friend Jerry would gladly share with anyone who is willing to listen that for him there are two incontrovertible truths he has learned in this life. They are: (1) His daughter born with Down's syndrome is his greatest blessing, and (2) the Lord is, indeed, his shepherd. The same, of course, can be said for countless men and women all over this globe. Like Jerry and I and, most dramatically, like the Apostle Paul, we have been so humbled by our arrogance and brought so low the pain forces us to look to God.

Another word in this introductory verse of Psalm 23 that deserves attention is the possessive pronoun "my." What the poet is pointing out through the use of this word is the startling reality that this Lord is not someone else's shepherd, is not even our shepherd, and is not some kind of generic shepherd, but is rather his or her own shepherd.

It is important to note here the difference between the definite article "The" as in of "The Lord" and what follows. In three words, the emphasis flows from impersonal to intimate as marked in the shift from "The Lord" to "my shepherd." The Lord may be, in the mind of the poet, an impersonal sovereign of everything, but this same Lord is also characterized as "my shepherd" and therefore as an intimate companion. This is a remarkable shift in emphasis from the detached sovereignty of God to an almost New Testament perspective of a God who enters into a willing intimacy with every receptive human being.

By proclaiming the Lord as my shepherd, this poet invites every reader to participate fully in the staggering reality that any believer can make the same audacious claim. Like the poet, we too can dare to utter these timeless words, "The Lord is my shepherd." If we so choose, we can permit them to mean to us exactly what I take them to mean to the poet, which is that this shepherd's presence pervades every dimension of our being.

The Lord, then, becomes my shepherd when I surrender so totally and so frequently that I permit holiness to guide me in every decision I make, from the establishment of personal boundaries to whether I participate in the latest gossip. The Lord is also my shepherd in every relationship I maintain. As a shepherd guides his sheep from behind, my shepherd directs me in my every decision from an unseen place as I make daily decisions affecting my wife and my daughter, family, friends, acquaintances, and even strangers.

The personal pronoun is a strangely penetrating word, and in the course of this first verse it establishes an uncompromising perspective that this poem, though written three thousand years ago, is still very much about me. As I read it, it is not about you. As you read it, it is about you and not about me. But in the process of pondering these words, I realize that this poem is about me and about God and about life as a process. It is also about hope and yearning, about necessary confrontations, about the threat of inevitable danger, and ultimately about a marvelous destiny. Most of all it is about the truth that whether or not I am aware of it, this God is sovereign over every detail that composes the sum of my life.

Some years ago, a pastor friend stood before his denomination's judicatory and offered what I believe to be one of the most profound statements I have ever heard. He was being examined by his fellow clergy in the process of moving into this body's geographical jurisdiction. By ecclesiastical law this man was required to read his prepared statement of faith. If the statement he presented was judged by his peers to be other than orthodox, he would be required to defend the tenets of his declaration.

On every other such occasion I have listened with less-than-enthusiastic interest since most such statements are, in my view, designed more to impress others than to express any authentic strivings with God. As one might expect, the more eloquent the statement the less likely questions will emerge from the floor of that august body. Consequently, most such presentations are tedious and sufficiently thorough so as to cover with at least a veneer of orthodox language every potentially controversial issue from the virgin birth to the bodily resurrection. What is more, each such statement is riddled with the ten-dollar words seminarians often use and only professors actually understand. Predictably these presentations are as long as they are boring.

But my friend's statement proved to be as startling as it was brief. He rose before the gathered members of this judicatory and read this prepared text: "I believe that Jesus Christ is my Lord and Savior even if I do not believe that Jesus Christ is my Lord and Savior." That was it. The learned (not to mention loquacious) members of this particular gathering had no idea what to make of such profundity accompanied by what I regarded as refreshing brevity, so no questions were posed. My friend sat down and was fully accepted into this new region of the denomination's life and ministry.

My thoughts regarding the first verse of this poem are similar to and are inspired by my brilliant colleague. Today I am willing to stand before any group and proclaim this publicly: "I am absolutely convinced that the Lord is my shepherd, even when I refuse, out of my strong allegiance to narcissism, to allow him to be my shepherd. And because he is my shepherd, the Lord is also your shepherd, and the shepherd of every man, woman, and child."

This is a sobering proclamation. This is also the best possible news we could receive, for as the remainder of the poem so eloquently informs us, this life is so constructed that every one of us needs a guide. We cannot make this journey alone. Most of us begin this life believing that we can, but the truth is that we cannot. I believe that three thousand years ago the poet discovered the truth that the Lord is indeed his shepherd out of some kind of painful setback. From this experience, the poet surrendered to one other than the self, and it was this one the poet regarded as sovereign over the whole of life. This poet, whoever he or she was, knew him as both an all-powerful lord to whom one must bow down and also as a gentle shepherd who employs subtlety to guide us where he would have us go. The psalm invites us, even compels us, to know him in exactly the same way.

One more important issue must be addressed here if we are to explore the full meaning of the intriguing image of a sovereign shepherd. It comes to us in the form of a subtle implication, and it must be couched in this question: If the Lord is my shepherd, what does that make me? There can be only one answer, and it is summarized in one less-than-flattering word—sheep. For it naturally follows that if the Lord is my shepherd, then I must be a sheep, or worse yet, even a lamb. So you are, along with the rest of humanity.

Most of us do not find it compatible with our egos to view ourselves as sheep. Once when I was leading a Bible study for several high school-age kids, I posed this question: "If you could be any animal, what would you be?" The answers were predictable: "I would be a cheetah!" one young man yelled out. A girl answered, "I would be a leopard." Another kid hollered, "I would be a shark." Another announced, "I would be a lion." And to the delight of everyone, a clever young man waited patiently for his window of opportunity before he yelled, "I would be a skunk!"

No one mentioned being a sheep. This was not at all surprising because sheep are by nature dependent creatures—wholly dependent upon the shepherd. And in this culture we are taught not to admire or even respect those who are dependent on others. So who in their right mind would ever think to view themselves as dependent sheep? The answer to the question is that possibly Israel's mightiest king saw himself to be just that.

But this poem does not promote dependence on other human beings. To the contrary, it proclaims the truth that the single, healthy, dependent relationship that any human being can experience is wholly with God. Dependence on other human beings is never a solution, while surrender to this Lord of the psalm, and the attendant dependence it implies, is the only path to genuine healing.

While we are prone to boast of eschewing dependent personal relationships, we form them regularly with other human beings, with chemicals, and even with all manner of fanciful dreams and illusions. Ironically, it takes the pain that protracted exposure to these relationships invariably generates for us to discover that the only dependent relationship that is ever really healthy is with the one whom the poet knows both as Lord and shepherd.

For without this necessarily dependent relationship with this sovereign shepherd, we are hopelessly lost, both as individuals and as a people. The prophet Isaiah recognized this to be true. Centuries after the poet first sings "The Lord is my shepherd," the prophet writes, "All we like sheep have gone astray; we have turned every one to his own way . . ." (Isa. 53:6).

Isaiah's proclamation is a concise summary of the human condition for all time. Our sad, bloody history is the tragic story of individuals, groups and nations who vainly attempted to make history without God. Without exception, every one of those efforts was doomed to failure. For the history of humanity has all too often been the tale of sheep gone astray, each one going his or her own way.

The genius of the first verse of Psalm 23 is that in five words the poet defines us as helpless, necessarily dependent sheep, describes with amazing accuracy God as both Lord (sovereign) and shepherd, and defines without either apology or equivocation the structure of the relationship between sheep and shepherd as one of absolute dependence.

That is a lot of freight to be carried in only five words. But what is just as intriguing is where the psalm next carries us, which I submit is to a promise most of us have little examined. To get there you must turn the page, but before you do that, remember that for us to inherit the promise that awaits us, we must first embrace as truth these five words: "The Lord is my shepherd." Without such an embrace, what lies ahead will be meaningless. But with those five words written upon our hearts, we can be assured that there is an inheritance awaiting us that we likely never permitted ourselves to believe was even remotely possible. This promise awaits us on the far side of fear—not because I say that it is there, but because a trustworthy shepherd has promised its presence. And three thousand years ago a genius, who was likely one of the first to discover it, was inspired by heaven to write these immortal five words, "The Lord is my shepherd."

Chapter II

I Shall Not Want

There are at least two possible interpretations of the four words "I shall not want." I will begin with what I perceive to be the culturally accepted view and then offer a second perspective, which points toward a much richer meaning that flows naturally from the idea of surrender.

What I learned from the cultural interpretation of "I shall not want" is a trite notion that experience has since taught me was pure myth. It goes something like this: Those who have confessed that the God of the psalmist is the Lord of their lives and who further embrace as truth the image of this sovereign as an intimate shepherd will somehow want for nothing because their earthly needs will be met if only they believe with sufficient faith.

After more than a quarter century of experience in the ministry, I have concluded that I have two serious problems with any perspective that peddles the principle that faith begets material abundance.

First, life's evidence belies this claim as false. Second, such a view seems to encourage shirking or passing the buck instead of assuming responsibility for one's own life and unwittingly to laud passivity as a virtue.

To buy into any interpretation that the strength of one's faith is the determining factor for abundance is tantamount to believing that I can not only control my own destiny but that I can also manipulate God. This is the height of vanity.

During my first year of seminary my favorite professor, a man who had just completed all of the requirements for his doctorate at Princeton, succumbed to a virulent form of cancer. He had waged the proverbial valiant fight for years, and he as much as anyone convinced me—not by his words but by his behavior—that the Presbyterian Church just might have something relevant to say to a tortured culture during that tumultuous decade known as the '60s.

In my second semester in seminary, he was taken to M. D. Anderson Hospital where, though a patient himself, he ministered to other victims of this disease, as well as to the physicians and other health care providers, with his inimitable wisdom and contagious wit. One man who seemed to care as much for this professor as I did informed me, following a prayer vigil in the seminary chapel, that if we, the seminary community, only possessed sufficient faith, our beloved professor would survive.

I felt angry and I was not certain what the anger was really about. I was too ill-informed and far too spiritually immature to make sense out of the feeling, so I wisely chose not to argue with this man's simplistic formula. I bolted from his presence after making an excuse for my sudden departure. All the way home to my apartment I fought against the tears, but once inside, I wept unashamedly. Some moments later an unexpected memory imposed itself upon my grief.

I recalled being in a theater in Dallas, when I was probably no more than six years old, enjoying Walt Disney's full-length animated version of "Peter Pan." In the course of that delightful children's tale Tinker Bell, the lovable little fairy, consumed a bottle of poison. Almost immediately, the light in her tiny being began to fade. The resonant voice of the narrator warned the audience that our beloved Tinker Bell was now surely dying and the single way to her full recovery was for us to clap and to clap hard. The voice further assured us that if we would clap with all our might, we just might save the precious little Tinker Bell. And clap we did. I probably have never clapped so hard, because suddenly I realized that I was responsible for this precious little fairy's life. Much to my relief, my fervent clapping worked. Within seconds Tinker Bell's light returned to its radiant glow. In my young mind I had escaped certain calamity.

Such a dynamic is fun for gullible children to believe, but soon enough we learned that whether or not we clapped, Tinker Bell's fate had been decided by the film's screenwriters. What I find fascinating—to the point of being disturbing—is how many intelligent adults still cling to the myth that if they just have enough faith, abundance, even if it is an abundance of good news, will surely come their way.

As far as I know, the entire seminary community prayed as earnestly as we knew how in the spring of 1970, and our beloved professor still died. I did not then believe, nor do I now believe, that had we only prayed more fervently our friend would have walked out of M. D. Anderson Hospital fully recovered. I honestly do not know why the man died. I simply know that we prayed and a gifted young man died.

We all wanted the professor to live. I did not know a person who knew him who did not want that. We desperately wanted him to live because we knew that there was so much he could have offered to us as students and as a church. But sadly, he died. Perhaps his death was God's mysterious answer to our prayers. I do not know how else to frame the tragedy of untimely death.

I gained a bit of wisdom from that grievous experience. A small part of what I learned is that when Psalm 23 informs us that "I shall not want," it does not mean that if we just have sufficient faith we will never be disappointed or that we will be somehow immunized against tragedy. This is not even close to what I believe the poet meant when he or she wrote "I shall not want."

Recently I happened upon a sticker attached to the rusty bumper of a pickup. It read: "Do not believe everything you think." What is wonderful advice: Just because we were brought up to believe in something in no way guarantees its veracity.

I was once commanded to discontinue the weekly lecture series I had begun in an affluent Dallas church because I had stated in the opening session that I believed that every so-called biblical business strategy for making money was nothing more than a hoax. What I meant was not to attack business ethics, but rather to indict against those who would peddle the myth that success measured by worldly standards is the product of a strong faith.

The next day the church's pastor called to "dis-invite" me to the church he served. I later learned that a man in the class I was teaching had authored a book concerning God's plan for our prosperity. Apparently this man's theology was tied to what I term the culturally sanctioned notion that if we just believe enough we shall not want for anything.

Some years ago I spent an incredibly hot week helping a crew of volunteers construct a small hospital in a *colonia* on the outskirts of Nuevo Laredo, in Mexico. Every afternoon the temperature on the roof of that building soared to at least 110 degrees Fahrenheit, causing those of us who were nailing down tar paper to escape every thirty minutes for water and rest breaks.

During one of those breaks, I remained on the roof and scanned a landscape scarred by unspeakable desperation. At the time as many as ten thousand families moved into this particular colonia annually, even though there was no electricity, no plumbing, and little else but misery, disease, and the hopelessness that invariably attends grinding poverty.

As I turned slowly 360 degrees, an enigmatic structure on the southern horizon caught my attention and gave me pause. At first I could not even begin to make out its odd shape. After several moments of squinting, I discovered on that distant rise a sight that for over a decade has caused me to ponder more questions than I have room to list. Out of nothing more than what appeared to be cinder blocks and scrap lumber the residents of the colonia were framing a cathedral. This was the skeleton of what was to be a huge cathedral, similar to those I had seen constructed of wood and adobe in other Mexican cities.

These people clung to life in no more than scrap wood and cinderblock boxes covered with tin roofs secured by nothing more than the weight of discarded tires. Yet there they were, beneath a scorching sun investing time and no small amount of passion in the cause of building an impressive church on the outskirts of desperation. It was as remarkable a sight as my eyes have ever beheld.

Every time I launch into one of my all-too-frequent bouts of self-pity, I reflect upon what I witnessed on that afternoon and it lends necessary perspective.

Of course I did not know these people who were building themselves a church. If questioned on the issue, however, I believe that to a person they would confess in their native tongue that the Lord is, indeed, their shepherd. What did they have to show for such faith? Actually, they lived with nothing more than hopeless poverty and the shell of a church that would never pass the municipal building code in any American city.

These people had earthly wants. To miss that point, one would have to be either asleep or so callused as to be incapable of compassion. Everything about their poverty pointed to needs—the need for plumbing, sanitation systems, schools, health care, adequate diets, jobs, police protection, and the list goes on. I have never in my life been in the midst of a people with more needs. Yet the primitive structure they constructed on the outskirts of the colonia spoke of a depth of faith and a courage that I have seldom if ever witnessed in our affluent churches in this country. Here were poor, illiterate peasants, thousands upon thousands of them, who, I suspect, would readily affirm and embrace these words, "The Lord is my shepherd; I shall not want."

How can they believe the psalm if they buy into our culturally conditioned principle that this passage has a correlative relationship between faith and fortune? The simple answer to that question is that they do not. Obviously they believe something else, or they would never go to the trouble of constructing a cathedral in a desert so unforgiving as to make any form of manual labor a serious health risk. I suspect that their long experience with wanting has taught them that this God whom they worship is not some celestial slot machine. God the shepherd may not shower them with earthly blessings, but next to their strong family ties, God is the only real hope they have ever known. To these humble folk, not wanting obviously means something very different than it means to those of us who have been raised in an affluent world. It is all too easy for us to get our perception of what we need tangled up with the illusion that if we have sufficient faith, God will bless us with things.

So if this passage is not about a correlation between faith and abundance, what is it about? The phrase suggests an axiomatic spiritual principle concerning the daily discipline of surrender. It first begins in one's thinking and then slips into the viscera; the ultimate consequence of daily surrender is that the natural human yearning turns from what Jesus called mammon to God—the source of all things.

While this phenomenon does not occur overnight, with time, patience, and daily practice of the discipline of aiming to make the Lord the absolute sovereign in one's life, the yearning for gods that can never heal much less save us from despair turns toward the source of all abundance—for God is, indeed, abundance.

Years ago following my move to central Texas, I was required by the governing ecclesiastical body to write my own brief statement of faith. I decided that sincerity punctuated by brevity was my best bet for dodging the barbs and arrows that clergy seem fond of hurling on such occasions.

I pondered the issue of my faith for probably no more than one-half hour, and then I wrote these words:

> My granddaddy was a sharecropper. My grandmother was a sharecropper's wife. My daddy was a sharecropper's son. I am the grandson and son of sharecroppers. Sharecropping is in my bloodline. And today, I stand before you as a simple sharecropper in that God owns everything. I do not own my own life or anything attached to it. God owns it all. God's Son, Jesus of Nazareth, is the Lord and Savior of this life and ministry that belongs wholly to God. That is what I believe.

While this statement was one of the briefest on record, next to my friend's, of course, I skated through the interrogation unscathed by so much as a single question. I have no way of knowing if those words contained any importance at all for anyone other than me. Like most human beings, I always dread standing before anyone to be interrogated. But in retrospect, I am grateful that I was compelled to write a clear statement of my faith, because in doing so I was almost overwhelmed with the absolute truth that this God we worship is the God of abundance.

Everything belongs to God. Everything! What surrender ultimately accomplishes is to bring us to this amazingly simple realization—everything is God's. Everything! Once we bump head first into this startling truth, our perceptual map of life is forever altered. One of the initial insights we gain in this process is that we begin to understand that this ONE we have learned to regard as the sovereign and personal shepherd of our lives is also abundance.

When we live with the illusion that our happiness is about the acquisition and possession of things, we are liable to adopt two spiritual errors that possess the power to torture us for a lifetime. They are: (1) Something besides God can heal us; and (2) as mentioned above, God will bless us with things and specific outcomes if we only have sufficient faith.

But the psalmist knew that the discipline of surrendering our lives to God would eventually, but certainly not overnight, take from a person his or her incessant yearning for everything save God. Said another way, if we steep ourselves in the abundance that is God, how can we possibly want?

The four words, "I shall not want" that compose part b of verse 1 are the natural consequence of what transpires in part a. It works like this: The poet recognizes who is Lord. A lord, again, is one to whom a subordinate submits and surrenders. As stated earlier, that is the only relationship between a lord who is the Lord's subject. Through surrender to God as Lord, this poet has discovered two astounding truths: (1) This Lord is a very personal, intimate shepherd, and (2) this sovereign-shepherd is also abundance in that the Lord is sovereign over all and the owner of everything. Consequently, the poet realizes that wanting for anything other than God is now nothing more than a fruitless distraction, because once a human being discovers the truth of God as abundance, wanting anything other than God would make no more sense than praying for rain in a downpour.

Abundance cancels out our want for the things of this world. But this abundance, which is God, is not limited to the material realm and, in fact, is more often expressed in spiritual blessing than in anything physical. Jesus not only understood this truth discovered by the psalmist one thousand years before his birth, he also lived it. In Luke's Gospel we read these words: "Foxes have holes, and birds of the air have nests; but the Son of man has nowhere to lay his head" (Luke 9:58).

Compare those words to how we live our lives today. Who among us can argue that Jesus lived the most abundant life of all? But Jesus, like the psalmist, discovered the principle that surrender begets an awareness of abundance that with time alleviates that chronic pain that is so much a part of our insatiable wanting.

Truth is something each of us must discover. This means that I cannot discover the truth for anyone other than for myself. Therefore, while Psalm 23 is the truth, it is the truth of another human being's experience; in that sense it is only a spiritual map. Consequently, it can be nothing more than a map of someone else's discovery. It is a very helpful, even eloquent map, but it is a map, nevertheless.

For any of us to discover what it means to live one day at a time with a genuine sense of serenity, we must first discover the truth that any authentic relationship with God requires surrender. Until we are willing to make that courageous step, we cannot possibly know God as our personal shepherd and we will inevitably live with the suffering that unrequited longing generates.

One of the most obvious growth industries in the city where I live is the storage business. Mini-warehouses seem to be popping up everywhere, like dandelions in spring. Although I live in a rural section of our county, on occasion I drive through Austin's suburban sprawl, some of which is aging while other parts are still under construction. As I observe houses through the front window of my pickup, almost without exception I note that every garage is so packed with clutter that there is scarcely room for the family automobile(s).

No wonder the storage industry is booming. To sum up in one sentence my experience of living in this affluent culture for more than a half century, I would say this: "We are a people who have been taught so well to want that we have learned equally well how never to be satisfied." These words are intended as an indictment of myself as well as of most Americans. The seemingly insatiable nature of our appetites and our ravenous pursuit of the idols that serve as the symbols of "the good life" are the primary causes of our suffering.

Human nature being what it is, our wanting can never be satisfied unless it takes us to the same place it took our ancient poet—to God. Wanting is that very human and subterranean force that drives us toward idolatry. In the main, idolatry is a more unconscious than conscious, not to mention insidious, exercise in futility that accomplishes little other than exacerbating our wanting. The more things we acquire in the vain attempt to satisfy our wanting, the more we seem to want. It is a vicious cycle that sadly possesses the power to destroy our spirit and to leave us loaded with possessions, and/or addictions. Eventually we find ourselves abandoned in an existential purgatory where emptiness and even a life-threatening despair may haunt us. We load up our lives with things, which in turn drag our spirits down.

Wanting itself is not a moral issue. In fact, it is a big part of what it means to be a human being. This wanting, or yearning, is every bit as prevalent in the church as anywhere else in the culture. Occasionally, as in the case of Saint Francis of Assisi, or in our modern experience with Mother Teresa, a saint comes along who lives out the spiritual path to inner peace discovered by the ancient writer of this psalm. These rare people have courageously embraced the simple but astounding truth that human beings can want for nothing, because through surrender they will discover the reality of God's abundance. Again, where there is abundance, there can be no wanting.

When I was in seminary decades ago, I was sad to discover that those of us who comprised the student body during the late '60s and early '70s had wants every bit as much as anyone

else. We wanted the best grades so that we might obtain prestigious positions. We wanted prestigious appointments at the
biggest churches possible so that we might make enough money
to support ourselves and our young families. We also wanted
the right connections so that we might get noticed as the next
rising star of our denomination as soon as possible. We wanted
acceptance and praise from our peers. We wanted and even told
ourselves that we needed almost constant recognition and
strokes from the faculty, so we vied with each other for grades.
We wanted to make a really big splash, so we wrote and polished
our best sermons and traveled to small churches where we tried
them out in the vain hope that someone just might pause long
enough at the front door following the service to tell us that
what we had delivered had been the best sermon they had ever
heard. We wanted to be included, so we believed what we were
taught was truth without questioning whether we really believed it. And we wanted to be saved from the despair of getting
lost in the shuffle, so we competed with each other to win one
of the graduate fellowships so that we might be guaranteed accolades upon graduation.

In my senior year I was, much to my surprise, elected president of the student body. It would be the only office for which I
would ever run. In reality, I did not even run for it—a friend
nominated me while I was away for a year on my internship in
Missouri. I returned to Austin to discover that I had been elected
president, an office which had far more to do with ceremony
than with any functional purpose.

One of the perks of the office, nonetheless, was to have my
photograph printed in an official publication of the seminary
prior to graduation. The effect of this small bit of notoriety was
negligible, but after my picture appeared in an insignificant
brochure, one of my classmates stopped me on a footbridge one
glorious spring afternoon. Initially, I thought that he was inter-

ested in visiting with me, but instead he hurled at me a volley of hurtful words aimed at convincing me that I was promoting myself over him in the cause of attracting the attention of a pulpit committee. I realized that arguing with this frightened man at the moment was of no more value than trying to convince a fence post to sing opera, so I waved him off and moved on in silent bewilderment.

The two of us never spoke again after that sad encounter. I have completely lost track of the man except that I heard he had gone to another state and made a tragedy of his ministry. What proved to be most sad is that on that day we ended a friendship because neither one of us was mature enough to embrace as truth the compelling reality that God is the personal, intimate shepherd of each of our lives. To borrow from the Scripture, we were also strangers to the truth that in total surrender to this sovereign shepherd there is release from all wanting that translates into a dramatic liberation from fear.

Had my colleague and I stopped to study this psalm and permitted it to guide of our lives, we both would have been far better off. The two of us, along with the rest of my class, had invested the last three arduous years studying the Bible in its original languages, as well as taking courses in theology, ethics, and all manner of pastoral subjects. Yet I suspect that neither one of us had any idea at that awful moment on the footbridge that the longing that flowed out of our fear was what was preventing us from loving each other.

We had no idea whatsoever of the truth. If I had been pushed back then to articulate any kind of interpretation of verse one of Psalm 23, I would have offered some amorphous statement that equated a sufficient faith in God with having all of our material wants satisfied.

Today I regard such thinking as seriously flawed. I am convinced that the evidence is far more weighted on the side of the perspective that maintains the end of wanting is the consequence of true surrender. I shall not want only because I have steeped myself in a long, disciplined, and intimate relationship with the shepherd of my life and of all life. Once I have practiced the difficult and, at times, seemingly impossible discipline of trusting God with everything, my wanting will begin to abate.

For those who have practiced this discipline for years, as it appears the poet did, wanting dissipates and may disappear altogether. Consequently, whoever wrote these eloquent words of verse one, "The Lord is my shepherd; I shall not want," discovered an important truth. The truth this poet uncovered is powerful enough to rid us of our most fundamental temptation—our desire to worship anything we believe might be capable of delivering us from fear.

Although staggeringly simple, the poet's truth is still so challenging that it feels close to impossible to realize. Nevertheless, it is the truth today every bit as much as it was the truth three thousand years ago when this genius wrote, "The Lord is my shepherd; I shall not want."

Inherent in those nine words is more comfort than any of us dreamed possible or could ever discover in the material things we chase after. What these words whisper across the ages is not that our voracious appetites will be finally satisfied, but rather that in the shepherd we will discover that wanting is nothing more than a habit that we can drop at any time that we are wise enough to do so. This is astounding news. This is also the most comforting but, at first glance, bewildering news that we could possibly hear. It is, however, wonderful news, even if we refuse to receive it as such and especially when we hear it from the perspective of being made to lie down in green pastures. For it is in those green pastures and beside still waters that our experience with the truth takes us to a new place within ourselves that we never knew existed, much less imagined we might be invited to explore.

Chapter III

He Maketh Me to Lie Down

A ll of Psalm 23 hinges on verse two. This audacious and, at first glance, bewildering declaration concerning green pastures, still waters, and restoration follows the three truths given to us in the first nine words.

> He maketh me to lie down in green pastures:
> he leadeth me beside the still waters.
> He restoreth my soul
> *Psalm 23:2-3*

Perhaps through some undisclosed crisis, the poet has discovered these truths: (1) God is the only true sovereign in this life to whom one must inevitably surrender; (2) this sovereign, who rules over every dimension of our existence, is also an intimate shepherd; and (3) the process of surrender chips away at the insatiable human condition of chronic wanting in that it grounds us, over time, in the core of abundance.

The second verse, the hinge of this psalm, is an amazingly succinct but eloquent commentary on prayer; it is also the link joining the three truths of the opening line with the drama that lies ahead. Without this prayer the pilgrimage cannot be continued, and without the restoration that the prayer promises, the three truths are forever lost. Then we are left to wander about aimlessly with nothing more trustworthy as a guide than the illusion that we are sovereigns of our own lives.

The poet seems to suggest that healing, or what we often term salvation, is a process and not a one-time event. In the writer's perspective, salvation is a process involving the daily discipline of surrender as opposed to the practice of some particular ritualistic formula. What he means by being made to lie down in green pastures is not an isolated occurrence. It is instead an inevitable part of the growth process or, more specifically, that always painful stretch beyond self absorption.

Although the poet has discovered and proclaimed the three truths, this wise person knows that every truth may only be safeguarded by earnest prayer. At first glance, the verse seems to have nothing at all to do with prayer. But with attention given to its rich imagery, it becomes clear that this passage is perhaps the most succinct statement in the whole of Scripture on the structure as well as the efficacy of prayer.

In this one verse the poet records the three acts of the shepherd: "He makes me lie down . . . he leads me . . . and he restores my soul." Each act is a distinct function of prayer, which is tied to the act of surrender.

The initial verb in the beginning of this verse is "make." Here, the poet is not declaring that the shepherd is inviting us to do anything. Neither is the shepherd offering a mere suggestion or granting us any real latitude in our own decisions. No, the verb is as clear as it is sobering. "He makes me lie down," the poet proclaims.

What does it mean to make someone lie down? Let us begin with the premise that all of us have at one time or another been made to lie down. Every one of us. As newborns and infants, our parents make us lie down for our own good—to sleep. After we mature, sometimes it is required of us metaphorically as well. We may not always be sufficiently conscious to recognize immediately that God is involved in this wrenching occurrence, but the truth is that every one of us has been made to lie down.

No adult is exempt from this painful experience. We are made to lie down, whether our lying down is the result of a major crisis in our life or whether we perceive it as a minor setback in our strategy for success. We are all made to lie down at some time in our lives.

I have been made to lie down so many times that I have lost count. In my own life the process of lying down has appeared most often in the form of a darkness that seems intent upon smothering my dreams like a wool blanket on a sultry night. Without exception, it happens in the wake of some major disappointment when my plans did not work out as I thought they might.

The depression arrives first in its cognitive form and hurls a barrage of nonsense at me regarding my inadequacy as a human being. Panic sometime follows. Fear is linked to shaming voices in my head that seem determined to torment me.

Is this darkness God's handiwork? There are two answers to that question. The first is yes and the second is no.

Yes, this suffering is God's handiwork in the sense that God is involved in every dimension of all of our personal reality (both conscious and unconscious). It is God's doing in the sense that, through the gift of free will, heaven permits us to be foolish enough to believe that we can function without God. So God is involved in the darkness that makes me lie down in much the same way that I witnessed the Acoma shepherd guide his sheep—from behind.

The answer also is no, in that the actual suffering that occurs is not God's intention for my life, or for any person's life except in the sense that pain becomes a tool in getting our attention as the first step in changing our perspectives. The ancient Greek word for repentance literally means to change one's way of thinking or to change one's mind. And the most effective incentive for such a change in human beings is pain. We are a stubborn and proud lot, and little else but pain is convincing enough to serve as a catalyst to change our perspective.

When I was a sixteen-year-old kid working on a ranch in the Texas hill country, I sprinted one moonlit night down a rocky hill in the wake of some mischief I had joined a buddy in fomenting. Unbeknownst to me, a rancher had strung three new strands of barbed wire across a stand of cedar posts that had not held a fence in years. That fence was strung as tight as a piano wire, and I impaled myself on barbs while running at sprinter's speed.

I awoke lying on my back with three distinct lacerations lining my chest and abdomen. This was no green pasture in which I was now lying. To my thinking God had nothing whatsoever to do with this being made to lie down except that the Almighty creates adolescent boys for mischief. I did make one sound decision on that painful night. I wisely decided never to run down that hill again.

In my adult life I have run into numerous metaphorical strands of barbed wire fences where, again and again, I have been made to lie down. God was involved, as the psalmist suggests, by virtue of heaven's gift of free will. On each one of those instructive occasions, however, what actually happened is that I collapsed under the weight of the decisions I had made, which had nothing to do with surrender and which were void of any genuine attempt at prayer. With each of those collapses, and only in retrospect, did I come to realize that the shepherd was pointing me toward a verdant pasture where necessary repose preceded a change of perspective.

Some years ago I was standing on the back of a boat casting my bait in the choppy waters of the Gulf of Mexico when a young man half my age posed to me a question I had heard before. He asked, "Do you know how to make God laugh?" I had forgotten the answer because I often choose not to remember the psalmist's first truth—the absolute sovereignty of God. Still determined to haul in a trophy redfish, I wagged my head in the direction of no. The young man said, "Tell him your plans."

A rigid allegiance to my personal agenda appears to be the mechanism God most often employs in knocking me down. As mentioned above, my plans without surrender and, I suspect, your plans without surrender, will, in the words of the psalmist, make us lie down as surely as thunder follows lightning. I think this is how the shepherd works. It may not happen for years, maybe not even for decades, but it will happen that eventually we will be made to lie down. And when it does occur, if we are wise enough, our prayers will change from the rote recitations of religion to an earnest, heartfelt, gut-wrenching cathartic, desperate plea for help from the only one who is powerful enough to lift us up.

What the psalmist is articulating here is the principle that unless we are down, the three truths enumerated in verse one will remain void of meaning and will lose all sense of urgency. As long as we insist upon being the object of our worship, our personal agendas will remain the map to our illusions of happiness. Consequently, the reality that God is the sovereign, intimate shepherd, and also the source of all abundance, will be nothing more to us than hollow words.

Without exception, every recovering addict I have ever interviewed has informed me that, in retrospect, it was through being made to lie down and rest in a green pasture that they had learned to be grateful for the pain that compelled them to begin their search for God. When any self-absorbed man or woman dares to take his or her eyes off of their own ego long enough to search for God, that individual begins to understand the full impact of what a psalmist discovered and wrote about three millennia ago. As I have stated throughout the first two chapters of this book, this psalmist maintains an unshakable position regarding the absolute sovereignty of God in all matters.

If we have spent any time at all in a church during our lives, we have likely become so accustomed to the familiar words in Psalm 23 that we fail to recognize that even though they were possibly written one thousand years before the birth of Jesus they offer a perspective somewhat unusual in the Old Testament. The psalm declares God's personal, even intimate, involvement in the life of every human being, instead of being invested only in the corporate life of Israel. Not until the revelation of Jesus Christ as God incarnate was such a perspective promulgated on a consistent basis.

Verse two appears to parallel both Jesus' perspective on the involvement of God in every person's life and on the efficacy of prayer. One question that surfaces out of this observation is: Was Jesus ever made to lie down? From the reading of the Gospels it is clear that he was, indeed, made to lie down, but the genesis of his experience was not the sin of idolatry as it is with us. Matthew's Gospel tells us in chapter four that "Jesus was led up by the Spirit into the wilderness to be tempted by the devil." After forty days, when he was exhausted and hungry, the tempter came to him and began his tricky dialogue attempting to entice Jesus to rely solely his own wits instead of trusting God as his sovereign. Jesus stood firm, even when the tempter quoted Holy Scripture in making his cagey argument regarding the virtue of self-reliance.

Jesus did not capitulate to the tempter because Jesus knew the truth discovered by the psalmist centuries before: that God is the only sovereign to whom every human being, even the Christ, must surrender.

The one who came to tempt Jesus in his condition of self-imposed hunger and physical weakness is known in this story by two names—the devil and Satan. In Greek the word "devil" is defined as that force that possesses the power to fragment us or to tear us to shreds. Satan literally means adversary, more explicitly, a hateful adversary. Each time I read the account of the temptation as it is recorded in Matthew's Gospel, I become even more convinced that what Jesus encountered in the wilderness was a close-to-unbearable inner terror, not some literal evil being with horns, a tail, and a pitchfork, tormenting him with grandiose possibilities. I offer this possibility because fear is what both names of this tempter suggest. Fear is what separates us from the ultimate truth of who we are as God's children created in the image of his love. Hatred or Satan, viewed as the adversary of love, is in reality nothing more than well-engineered fear.

The lesson illustrated in this story of Jesus' temptation by fragmentation and by hate is simple yet instructive. Its point is that we are free to embrace as ultimate truth what the psalmist and Jesus both discovered. We may trust God as the absolute sovereign of our lives or we may wander about through the whole of this existence operating under the falsehood that we are the masters of our own lives. In making this more unconscious than conscious decision, we invariably point ourselves in the direction of being made to lie down in verdant pastures so that we might finally pause long enough to look up and then, perhaps, discover the truths expressed so succinctly in the first verse.

Do these types of trials and watershed events happen to all people? While I think that being made to lie down in green pastures does, indeed, happen to all adults, it appears that only a few of us proud human beings ever really come to the place of embracing as reality all three of the psalmist's truths. We are so fortified with rationalizations that we seldom allow the truth of God's sovereignty to penetrate our defenses. Fear drives us and works to fragment us from ourselves and to separate us from the truth. Whether it be foolish pride, all-out ignorance, spiritual immaturity, a trenchant and unconscious dedication to remaining fear's victim, or a combination of all of the above, the chronic nature of fear still prevents some people from seeing the truth. These folks seem to languish for a lifetime in an unhealthy cycle of being knocked down or, in the words of the psalmist, being made to lie down over and over again without gaining so much as one glimpse of self-awareness.

The agonizing consequence of this cycle is that those who adamantly refuse to heed the gift of being "made to lie down in green pastures" will at almost any cost avoid knowing God, because what they have made of their lives is a lie. This may sound like a harsh, seemingly condemnatory statement, but it is the truth, nevertheless. Mark Twain wrote, "You can't pray a lie." Expanding upon his assertion, I would add this: You also cannot live a lie free from serious consequences. As long as we deceive ourselves into believing that we need not surrender to God, we live a lie. The consequence of this lie is that we will be made to lie down repeatedly until such time that we become willing to change our minds in the cause of giving up the lie and surrendering to God.

The single force powerful enough to liberate us from the lies we manufacture is prayer. And the nine words of the first verse, though they are some of the most eloquent, not to mention insightful, ever penned, do not in and of themselves possess the power to liberate us. While they are indeed the truth, we must first experience fully what it means to be made to lie down where we might rest and, if we are wise, reflect upon how it is that we ended up flat on our backs. It is only from this experience that we ever come to understand that being made to lie down is an amazing act of love. If we heed its message, it might well become the initial step in our long journey toward joy—sometimes love hurts.

When we are so immersed in ourselves that we become lost, the shepherd has a way of showing up to lead us to green pastures where he makes us lie down. This allows us to gain the perspective that a fundamental change in our thinking requires. Later he takes us from those verdant fields of hope and leads us to a sacred place where our prayers might first be framed and then uttered—that is, once we have mastered God's language. This place where he now leads us is beside still waters. It is a world of silence. There is not even so much as a ripple or a splash in these waters. The shepherd knows that earnest prayer—the kind necessary for the restoration of our souls—always requires silence.

Perhaps the same poet who wrote Psalm 23 also penned these words found in Psalm 46, verse ten: "Be still, and know that I am God." As these words suggest, the still waters in Psalm 23 are, next to Jesus' lesson on prayer, the most helpful words in the whole of Scripture in teaching us how to pray. The writers of these two psalms have discovered yet another secret about God that is shared so subtly that unless—we slow down and ponder these words—we will surely miss. The secret is that God's language is silence.

Our language, it seems, is noise: cacophony, clamor, and chatter. The shepherd knows this. That is why he comes to us after we have rested in green pastures. He reaches out to us and then delivers us to another place where we might learn to converse in his language. It would make no more sense to travel to central Mexico and attempt to converse with a Spanish-speaking farmer in English than it would to impose upon heaven our native tongue. If we are to converse with God in the sincere hope of experiencing the restoration of our souls, we must first learn to speak God's language of silence.

It is not a difficult dialect at all. There is no challenging vocabulary to commit to memory, and it is not driven by irregular verbs. It is a simple language that even a very young child may learn. At first glance, this language appears so simple that we deceive ourselves into believing that there will be nothing to our mastery of it. But while God's language is simple, it is not easy. God's language is silence, and silence is a terribly difficult discipline for us to master.

This is what I have learned about prayer since I, too, was made to lie down and rest so that I could be led to the still waters: Prayer has far more to do with listening than with speaking. That insight does not surprise me. A friend of mine, a psychologist, told me that 75 percent of what we remember from any conversation is what we ourselves have said. If this is true, and I believe that it is, it makes sense that if prayer is about speaking, what we will likely take away from the experience is little more than a sense of pride regarding our eloquence.

Some time after the poet wrote of still waters as the locus of prayer, the prophet Elijah bumped into the identical truth. According to the writer of I Kings, he searched for God in a wind, an earthquake, and a fire, and then he discovered God in "a still small voice," or what I am told by a Hebrew scholar might be translated as "a silence that was so profound that it actually spoke."

We have so filled up our minds with chatter and also with the constant cacophony of the culture that we find it almost impossible to become quiet. Some years ago I experienced a particularly stressful week that culminated in the necessary euthanasia of my daughter's beloved cat. While I am not particularly fond of cats, I had grown to like this magnificent tom who exhibited a tender confidence that was merely one rung on the ladder below arrogance. To my shock, this beloved creature developed a virulent form of leukemia and suffered so that "putting him to sleep," to employ the standard euphemism, became the only option.

Hours following the unpleasant chore of delivering the cat to the vet, I accepted the invitation of a Buddhist friend of mine to join his community for an hour of lecture followed by a half hour of meditation. My long experience in the church had trained me to listen well and I absorbed much of the material in this fascinating discourse on the several parallels between American Protestantism and Buddhism. Following the lecture, my friend sounded a tiny, resonant bell, and the group began to meditate.

Because such a practice is foreign to my tradition where more than two minutes of silent prayer is considered "dead time," I became immediately restless. I listened as the ceiling fan clicked above my head with each revolution of its long blades. Next I turned my attention to the rising crescendo of the cicadas' summer hymns on the far side of the open windows. These sounds of summer brought memories attached to those days before the advent of air-conditioning closed off our senses to the world beyond our window panes.

Memories are not what meditation is about, but I found it difficult and close to impossible to turn down the chatter in my head. As fervently as I searched, I could not seem to locate the "off" switch. One inane conversation after another raced through my thinking like some audiotape turned to fast forward. Over and over I thought of the cat I had put to sleep that day: with each rehearsal of that sad memory I could feel myself on the threshold of sobs, but not so much as a tear dared show itself.

Somewhere near the end of that half hour of silent meditation, and after I had secretly checked my watch several times, I suddenly realized that I was now traveling to a place within myself where I seldom allow myself to venture. I possess no name to hang on this remote corner of my being except to know it as depth. I was now so deep into wherever it was I was journeying, more by mystery than by any plan on my part, that I left behind all grief concerning the cat and, moments later, all thoughts at all. The chatter hushed like birds before a thunderstorm and the cacophony of life—the radio music with which I clutter my mind when I tire of thinking, the honking of automobile horns, the roar of the freeway, even the pleasing arpeggios sung by a host of summer cicadas—suddenly disappeared. Beneath a whirling ceiling fan that I could no longer hear, I discovered myself alone in a silent place where I felt not the least bit uncomfortable.

All too soon my Buddhist friend again rang the bell, and I was aware of feeling unexpected resentment. I had no desire to leave the place where mystery had led me. The last thing I longed for in that moment was to face the grief I had abandoned and return to a world of racket. The cicadas seemed more raucous than before, and the gentle rattle of the ceiling fan came close to hurting my ears.

Everything in me yearned to return to the place I had just abandoned, but the mystery had vanished and for the life of me I could not figure out how to retrieve it or how to get back to it. As I rose from my place on the floor, I felt the near-chronic ache in my back return as though someone was pushing a sharp blade into my spine. I could feel the familiar tension etching itself into the features of my face, and my thoughts began to bounce back and forth like a pinball from one future obligation to the next.

Through the practice of daily meditation, I have learned the name of the place I visited. I am convinced that whether we approach it via a Christian path or a Buddhist path or a Jewish path or some other path, its name remains the same and it is simply called "still waters." It is at this still and serene place where, when we finally dare to silence the aggregation of inner voices that vie for our attention and our allegiance, authentic prayer happens.

Authentic prayer occurs when we dare to be quiet and become so reverent that we listen for God. What I came to realize on my evening with the Buddhist congregation is that prayer is at least 99 percent listening for God and to the silence of God's language and no more than 1 percent speaking to God.

Of course we need to speak to God as we would speak to a loving, intimate father to whom we are willing to entrust everything. When Jesus taught his disciples to pray, he taught them a very economical prayer. He taught them essentially to cover the bases that needed covering. Beyond that, I believe silence is our most efficient prayer.

I pray in airports, while driving, in restaurants, in meetings, and anywhere else I pause long enough to recognize that I need to utter a few sentences to my heavenly Father. Mostly these are sincere offerings, but I find it impossible to listen for God when I am distracted. This is why the poet tells us that the sovereign shepherd comes to us when we have been made to lie down and leads us to a place beside still waters. Stillness is the venue where we can most often hear God. Hearing God, as opposed to chatting with God, is the process that mysteriously restores us from hopelessness to obedience, from chaos to discipline, from self-recrimination to self-acceptance, from sadness to laughter, and from tears to joy.

This is exactly how the psalmist describes God's promise. From a prone position of bewilderment and repose in green pastures, you and I are promised that we will be led by the shepherd to a place of stillness where the soul will be restored.

I believe this means that the soul remains that indefinable part of us that is always connected to God, even when we do not realize that we are linked to holiness. The truth of the soul is that we can no more escape our relationship to God than we can escape ourselves. We are inextricably tied to God, and the soul is the invisible link that binds us to mystery.

If we think or speak of the soul at all, most of us regard the word as some archaic metaphor that sounds more romantic than talk of the subconscious and less clinical than the terms employed in any in-depth discussion of psychology. Those who would relegate the word soul to some bygone nomenclature commit a serious error, because the soul is as real and every bit as meaningful today as it was three thousand years ago when the poet wrote of the possibility of its restoration.

A physician friend of mine once told me that when the technology we today know as radiology was invented in the nineteenth century, the medical community actually believed that the soul would show up on x-rays. Such a naive perspective might strike us as quaint. But that the soul remains hidden from view does nothing to obviate its reality.

How do we define this soul that the poet informs us stands in need of restoration? I do not really know the answer except to suggest that it has much to do with a right—and by that I mean surrendered—connection with God. Other than that, I really do not know how else to define it. I believe that it is likely more than our connection or relationship with God, but I also know that my relationship with God, and consequently with myself and the world, is that part of me that stands in sore need of the restoration.

In simplest terms, what I glean from the imagery of still waters and restoration is the real-life experience of deciding again and again that if I am ever to become wise and relatively peaceful, I must surrender everything to God. Surrender occurs sometime after an experience in green pastures and at a place called "still waters." I know this to be my truth, and I see it to be the truth of the psalmist as well. Our souls may be restored only by prayer, and prayer is that mystery whereby we come to our senses only because we come home to God.

What is so fascinating about all of this is that, inspired by God, the poet knows that this God we seek is also always seeking us. Even when we do not know what it is that we need, heaven always knows. Consequently, when we cannot go on, when life on our terms no longer makes any sense to us, when our dreams have been blown about by the storm winds of disappointment, the shepherd appears and provides us with exactly what we need.

Today we know this generous provision as the process and also the arena for every authentic prayer that has ever been uttered from the lips of a human being. The process of prayer begins by our being made to lie down flat on our backs in green pastures. It is in this place that we decide finally to open our formerly closed minds to the possibility of real change. Once we do that, the shepherd appears to lead us to a place so quiet that God's language is the only reality. Here we are restored to an effective connection with God, and also to a right relationship with ourselves and to the whole of creation.

This process of prayer is the only sufficiently powerful way to communicate the truths we learned from the poet in verse one, and it is also the requisite for all that lies ahead.

The truths have been set forth, the prayer has been experienced, and now we are equipped to take the journey that God would have us make and for which an ancient poet has provided a map. But the prayer is not done: if we are to maintain a firm grip upon the truth, the prayer can never be done.

Chapter IV

He Leadeth Me

E mboldened by truth and stirred by the mystery of prayer, we dare to follow the shepherd into adventure. With him as our guide, we find ourselves willing to step into the marketplace and into our professional and personal relationships with a new perspective that encourages us to focus on just one thing—doing what is right. Prior to our encounter with the shepherd, and for the whole of our lives before the perspective we gained by being made to lie down, we mainly wanted to be right. Long before we found ourselves in a place where we might learn for the first time what it means to listen, we were far more invested in being right than we were interested in doing what is right.

he leadeth me in paths of righteousness
for his name's sake.
Psalm 23:3

After our time of prayer, we change our minds about many things, and we are not certain what to make of this shift in attitude. But being right no longer possesses the power it once held over our every decision. To our astonishment, we find ourselves dedicated to doing what is right rather than in proudly working to convince ourselves and the world that we are right. These are not the only results of the process we have experienced at the shepherd's gentle hand. We no longer find ourselves interested in demonstrating how impressive we are, and nor does the lime-light have the appeal it once held for us.

If someone in the crowd does single us out, point in our di-rection, and comment aloud on the change they see in us, we do not give it much thought because we have come to care very little about what others think of us. Everything in us is now changing due to our daily surrender to the one whom the poet has taught us to call Lord. We are no longer so attracted to the myriad of insidious lies that once drove us to the brink of ex-haustion. Our only attraction is to the truth and yet, in the early stages of being set on these paths of righteousness, we find ourselves bewildered as we stumble about struggling to differentiate lies from the truth. This is not an easy process, but we remain determined for we know that we are now on the right path.

Because we are so accustomed to the lies that have claimed us for years, we find that we must be very careful. The pride that earlier fueled our downfall and brought on difficult defeats through which we discovered our authentic selves can easily in-fluence us to make doing what is right one more exercise in self-aggrandizement.

Such is the insidious nature of pride. The poet anticipates this in the artful structure of the psalm. The writer knew that human nature being what it is, the next natural step would be for us to dedicate ourselves to doing what is right for all the wrong reasons.

This is why the psalmist describes the process immediately following the prayer as being led in paths of righteousness for his shepherd's name's sake. This is an important, even crucial, part of the psalm. It reminds us that if we are left to our own de-vices, we will do what is right for the sake of our own reputations or personal gain rather than choosing righteousness as a witness to the one who is righteousness.

During the time Psalm 23 was written, uttering the name of God was viewed to be synonymous with evoking the presence of the deity, the one whose name was considered far too holy for human beings to pronounce. This equation holds interesting implications for our interpretation. In simple terms, whenever we do what is right we are witnessing God's presence in the world. Therefore, any righteous act on our part that is consciously done for "his name's sake" liberates us immediately from self-absorption. It becomes a manifestation of God's will being expressed through us, as opposed to one more attempt on our part to be noticed.

It is obvious to us now that the shepherd has placed us on the right path. But for us to remain here we must become vigilant to the almost overwhelming temptation to enhance our own reputations or to seek the praise of others through our daily demonstrations of doing what is right.

Doing the right thing for the wrong reasons is something we have all done. I know that I have been the cause of more than one disaster. When I arrived in Dallas in April 1975 to serve on the pastoral staff of a downtown church, I heard as a recurring theme in the murmuring of that congregation these words: "I wish we could return to the good old days when we had thirty-five hundred members and the likes of Billy Graham came here to preach."

In the mid-'70s, this church had on its bloated rolls around two thousand members, but the actual membership was closer to half that number. The church's dynamic pastor at the time, Dr. John F. Anderson Jr. was fond of saying, "There is no such thing as a bad church location; we just have to figure out what it is good for."

In my view it did not take a rocket scientist to figure out that the most faithful decision this congregation could make would be to turn their thoughts from the grandiose illusions of yesteryear so that they might, in the words of the prophet Amos, refocus their energy on letting "justice roll down like waters, and righteousness like an ever-flowing stream" (Amos 5:24).

After hearing their confusion and taking to heart the senior pastor's proclamation about there being no such thing as a bad church location, I set about to do what I deemed necessary to lead these people in the direction of Amos's words. What I deceived myself into believing I had accomplished was nothing short of remarkable. In fact, I convinced myself that my decade of service put this old downtown church on the map, and arguably granted them their *raison d'etre* to remain in their historic, once prestigious location in downtown Dallas.

Eight months after I arrived I embarked on a venture with another, more seasoned associate pastor that would forever alter my perspective on life. During the final week of October this man and I, along with three volunteers, opened a soup kitchen where we fed approximately forty homeless men and women in a church hallway. The volunteers warmed several pans of canned vegetable beef stew on a small electric range, and I opened the door and welcomed that first small, bedraggled group of homeless men and women to our fledgling soup kitchen in the name of Jesus Christ.

Ten years later, when I left the church, the soup kitchen had approximately $400,000 in the bank and had—under my leadership—so expanded its contribution base that it generated close to $500,000 in income annually. At that point the ministry was feeding, on average, three hundred men, women, and children daily.

From that mustard seed we expanded our ministry to include an apartment building where homeless families could live rent-free for ninety days, a state-of-the-art battered women's shelter, a free-standing all-night shelter for the homeless, an advocacy and psychotherapy program for women incarcerated in the Dallas

County Jail, a summer day camp for the children from the most desperate neighborhood in Dallas, and various other programs.

Being a part of the founding and development of those ministries marked the most exhilarating period of my career: in truth, it was a heady time. I often pinched my arm when I found myself meeting with the so-called movers and shakers of the city, and I was invested in garnering as much of the media spotlight as possible as I spoke regularly on behalf of the homeless.

I abandoned that position and all that I had deceived myself into believing that I had founded because, in truth, I never fit into that congregation. They are good, even wonderful people, but our worldviews were poles apart. Retrospectively, I know that after the first six months in their midst I realized that both they and I had made a mistake in the pastoral relationship we had established.

Be that as it may, I doubt that anyone could find much to criticize in one of those programs. They were pure and amazingly simple and, therefore, not surprisingly effective. Most are still in operation, and the soup kitchen has even been expanded and is now housed in its own building.

A few years ago the soup kitchen, which is known as "the Stewpot," marked its twentieth anniversary. I was disappointed to hear from a former colleague that I was not to be invited to celebrate the founding of a ministry that has become recognized nationally as one church's faithful approach to ministering to the homeless. Upon hearing that discouraging word, I pouted for perhaps as much as a day and then drowned my sorrow in a cup of cappuccino and decided in favor of every cliche my mind could manufacture in the cause of letting bygones be just that.

Some weeks later another friend who had also been instrumental in the establishment of the programs reported to me that the church had published some kind of "Christmas letter" proclaiming the anniversary of the ministries and telling the story about what I still consider to be their somewhat miraculous beginnings.

According to my friend, nowhere in that brief historical sketch was my name even mentioned. Here I had invested ten arduous years of my life on the streets of Dallas. I had been knocked out once by an angry man and had also been chased at night by a gun-wielding thug who threatened to kill me because I had refused him admission to the soup kitchen. On another occasion a man had thrown a brick at me, grazing my head. The evening before the morning I was scheduled to stand before the Dallas City Council with a request for a zoning variance so that we might found a battered women's shelter, I received a phone call from a man who threatened to kill my daughter if I did not rescind my proposal. From my point of view, I decided that I had more than paid my dues and had virtually nothing more to show for those amazing ten years than scars inflicted by well-intentioned Christians, some of whom fought me every step of the way as I took one risk after another in what I convinced myself was the bringing to incarnation the compassion of Jesus Christ.

Armed with this latest bit of self-righteousness, I decided to be livid with people I had not even laid eyes on in more than a decade. In fact, I all but ruined three whole days of Christmas vacation resenting the fact that I did not get the credit that I was absolutely sure was due me. Two days after Christmas in 1995, I took a long walk alone as the winter sky threatened rain, if not more substantial precipitation. I donned a sweater, plopped a comfortable cap on my bald head, and trudged off into what I was certain would be another hour of a one-sided conversation with God about not receiving my just due.

Somewhere during that walk, I heard a voice. To be sure it was my voice, but it was not spewing the vile rage I had been ranting for days. Unlike any time since I had been told of the great slight to my reputation, I heard a voice whispering a bizarre notion in my head. It began by stating that God had been given plenty of credit. I could only agree. Then it posed this question: "Who do you think really made those programs go, you or God?" I grinned into the cold wind as I mumbled the truth in this one word—"God." "Well then," the voice continued, "God got the credit he is due, so why are you so ticked off?" At that point I could only laugh, and the laughter came out of the recovering part of me who daily surrenders to God and then all too often slides about on the slippery slope of narcissism.

When I thought I was founding those programs, I had no idea whatsoever what it meant to surrender. Though I was a seminary graduate, I had never encountered the concept of total surrender to God. Or if I had, I missed it completely. In truth, the church culture participated no small amount in convincing me that my ministry and my life were pretty much up to me. The seminary, as I mentioned earlier, was every bit as competitive as my undergraduate program, where in the mid to the late '60s we were literally studying for our lives to stay out of the draft. As the Vietnam War heated up, only those males who remained in the top half of their undergraduate class were exempt from being called into the armed services. Once that sobering news reached our tiny campus in North Texas, most of us buckled down to the serious business of not only remaining in college, but of living with the vain hope that the war might blow over before we graduated.

Once I was in seminary, I realized how this game of ministry was played. Oh, to be sure we gave lip service to the sovereignty of God, but it did not take long for every one of us insecure entering students to realize that, while the sovereignty of God was a sound doctrine, not to mention a necessary conviction if we ever hoped to be ordained, the real opportunities lay with those who took good care of themselves by excelling in the classroom.

We developed a pseudo-community that was covered by a thin veneer of piety and feigned personal concern for one another but which, in reality, was predicated upon the same human insecurities that breed self-centeredness in secular contexts.

What we accomplished we most often did for our own self-aggrandizement, with the hope that the good reputation we began in seminary might serve as the seeds for glorious careers. Thirty years ago few of us would have dared to examine our motives, but our unspoken belief might best be summarized in a pithy and culturally sanctioned message that placed us in position for a head-on collision with any doctrine concerning the sovereignty of God. That message was: "If it is going to be, it is up to ME!"

While I never recall actually uttering those words, this message became so embedded in my unconscious that I gave it tacit permission to make me sick. It, more than any other message, drove me from the truth that the psalmist discovered three thousand years ago: that all righteousness must be accomplished for the shepherd's name's sake.

It is now embarrassing for me to confess that I had, until recently, never made the connection between my narcissism and my conviction that my ministry and even my life were entirely up to me. The consequence of this error was that I did many right things for the poor of Dallas, but for the wrong reasons.

One unusually hot September afternoon following my ten years of service to the homeless, I sat in the office of a Dallas psychiatrist, who himself was an ordained minister. The man posed to me what I thought at the time an odd question. He asked, "What caused you to open a soup kitchen?"

At first I was taken aback by the man's obvious stupidity. How could he ask me such a thing, I wondered. Had he not read the papers and seen the reports on television concerning the burgeoning population of homeless people since the deinstitutionalization of the mentally ill in Texas in the late '60s? Recognizing that there was probably far more to this question than met my eye, I offered this cautious response: "Because they were hungry."

He gazed at me and said, "Maybe, but I think there is another reason."

"What is it?" I asked.

Without hesitation, he stunned me with his answer. "I believe it was because you were hungry."

"Me? Hungry? Doc, I have never been hungry in my life!"

"Not for food," he half whispered. "No, you were not hungry for food, but you were starved for recognition."

The words stung only because they were true. I heard them, accepted them as possibly accurate, but it was more than ten years later that I discovered the insidious nature of my narcissism and also bumped into the veracity of God's sovereignty as contained in these ancient words, "he leads me in paths of righteousness for his name's sake."

"His name's sake" is the only predicate for sanity in living this life. If I have discovered anything worth sharing with others in the past half century, it is this: The only healthy way to live is to eliminate as much as possible our self-absorption from the equation and focus our energies entirely upon what it means to love. This, in my view, is exactly what it means to walk the path of righteousness "for his name's sake."

If we do what is right, we will be centered in love, and if we love, we will no doubt be doing what is right. But any demonstration of love must be surrendered wholly to God. This is also what it means to be led in paths of righteousness for his name's sake. I have done some right things, but unwittingly I did them for the sake of my own reputation or personal gain, and in the process sowed the seeds of misery. Today, however, by God's grace I realize, that all true righteousness begins invariably with a total, but still imperfect, surrender to God.

When I am called upon to teach, I now focus on the students and on my perception of their need to hear the truth of God's love for them. Next I focus on what I perceive the truth to be as I expound on it from the Scriptures. This is an arduous process drawing on the training I received in the seminary. Then, in the moments before every teaching or preaching event, I make the following my sincere prayer: "Lord God, please get me out of the way today so that these people might hear your truth and know more about you and even less about me."

I do not offer this prayer out of any false sense of self-efface-ment: I make it my petition because I now realize how much I crave attention and seek to be the star. It is also out of this hon-est perspective that I know I must remain focused on the daunt-ing challenge of doing what is right in this life, not for my reputation's sake, but rather for the sake of God's holy name.

The simple but profound reason that I make this prayer is be-cause I have come to believe that this ministry with which I have been entrusted by God is not at all about me. It never really was. But years ago, while I knew the words of the psalm backwards and forwards, from the depth of my soul I was convinced that God had called me to be impressive and that together God and I would make one huge splash that would show up in the head-lines of the *Dallas Morning News*.

I now realize I was dreadfully mistaken and that the poet held the secret all along. This life is not about self-importance and neither is my ministry about reputation. What I am called to do is always about God, and the only way to be about God is to leap faithfully with both feet into the paradox of permitting ourselves to be led down the paths of righteousness by getting completely out of the way. At first glance, this does not seem to make much sense, but then a paradox never does. This paradox did not make any sense to me for most of my life. Today, however, I embrace the words of the psalmist about being led in paths of righteousness for "his name's sake" as the single path to sanity. It is without question a counter-cultural view, and every time we align ourselves with righteousness for the name sake of the shepherd, we will find ourselves in a distinct minority.

Unfortunately, our culture teaches us from the very beginning, even in the church, to operate out of a sense of our own name's sake. Early on we are taught to do the right thing for the sake of our own reputation, or for the sake of family loyalty, school pride, or patriotism. Seldom if ever are we instructed by our cultural institutions, even the institutions of the family, church or synagogue, to embrace the secret of the psalmist and to permit ourselves to be led on the path of righteousness for the sake of the shepherd's name.

The single place in this culture that I have ever discovered such a notion is in the twelve step meetings I have attended regularly for the past five years. Without knowing exactly what I was looking for, I searched for such a perspective for the whole of my ministry in the institutional church. What I discovered in the church most often, however, was the struggle for power, the exaltation of the self, and small personality cults, most of which were veiled in pseudo-piety and couched in religious language.

Close to exhausted and burned out after attempting to keep alive a church-related, non-profit corporation that my instincts told me I should have allowed to die a natural death from the first day I took the reins, I happened into an Alcoholics Anonymous meeting in a church basement. I am not powerless over alcohol and I have never ingested an illegal drug in my life, but on that morning I was desperate for some kind of solace. My soul was drowning in fear and I knew nowhere else to turn.

The experience was what I needed. A man immediately across the table from me opened the meeting with this brief testimony: "I have forty-plus years in this program, and today I am no longer afraid."

Those words were precisely what I needed to hear. But the man was not finished. He startled me with these surprising words: "The Lord to whom I surrender every day did it all. I did nothing and can do nothing without him."

In modern parlance, this is the simple but costly principle the psalmist is inviting us to embrace. Because of the wonderful gift alcoholism finally becomes to those who discover surrender, this man had also unexpectedly bumped into the identical truth that had transformed a poet's thinking three thousand years ago. In particular, surrender to the Lord produces in us a transformation that leads us to the path of doing the next right thing, strengthened by the awareness that anything we might accomplish is evidence of God's power.

Outside of what is today known as the "Recovery Movement," I seldom bump into such a perspective. In my own experience there are a few pastors and a handful of lay persons who hold to such a view. In my career as a pastor I have all too often found organized religion to have more interest in being right than in doing what is right for his name's sake. I realize that this is a cynical view, and if I thought it would do any good, I could list example after disappointing example as evidence to support my position.

I refrain because I have discovered I do not need to fix anything or to invest much energy pointing out the faults of others, even of the church I have struggled to love for most of my life. I have learned from the psalmist that all I need to do is to keep my feet on the path of righteousness and give credit to the Lord.

It is easy to discern from the book of Acts that a man named Saul honestly believed that he was doing the right thing. As he traveled up the road to Damascus to round up the followers of Christ and return them to Jerusalem bound in chains, Saul was committed to doing what was right by his own definition of righteousness.

But the one the psalmist calls Lord had other plans for Saul. As Saul traveled toward Damascus intending to inflict righteous violence, Christ knocked him down and ultimately sent him toward the identical discovery made by the writer of Psalm 23. Namely, that the only appropriate relationship a human being may enjoy with God is one of absolute surrender.

Saul was blinded by the light on the road to Damascus. In his letter to the church in Galatia, which he wrote years later, he tells of spending three subsequent years in Arabia. We do not know the details of what occurred in those years, but I believe that a big part of what he accomplished was to learn the life-changing secret of surrender. The most amazing testimony to this man's change of mind, or conversion, is contained in his second epistle to the church at Corinth. In that letter he writes, "My (God's) power is made perfect in weakness" (12:9). In my view, there is not a discernible difference between this statement and the psalmist's proclamation that "he leads me in paths of righteousness for his name's sake."

If we embrace both declarations as truth, they liberate us from the need to impress others. These two statements also deliver us to a whole new way of life. Like the psalmist, we get out of the way so that the shepherd's name might be glorified: like the apostle, we become willing to boast of our weaknesses. Precious few of us are ready to consider, much less embrace, such an attitude, but those of us who have been made to lie down and who have been taught to listen have learned that this life is far more about how we love than it is about what others think of us.

Once we learn this important lesson, everything changes. But this conviction does not come to us easily nor does it remain with us simply because we will it to stick around. The truth only arrives and stays with us because through pain and surrender we finally decide to trust everything to mystery. The result of such courage is that for the first time in our lives we learn and live the highest possible definition of love. The great lesson we take from the experience is that everything about us belongs to the one the psalmist called "my shepherd," especially the credit for turning our thinking from self-absorption toward the genuine humility that over time delivers us to a path called righteousness.

Chapter V

Yea, Though I Walk
Through the Valley

We have now discovered the first great lessons of the psalm, and it is likely that we have embraced them more as theoretical truths than as visceral reality. We now recognize, intellectually at least, (1) that the Lord is sovereign, (2) that this sovereign is our intimate shepherd, and (3) that surrender to this Lord will permit us to chip away at our condition of consistent longing for any deity we believe will relieve our pain.

We have been made to lie down by the shepherd who loves us enough to conspire with our poor decisions to bring us to our knees in some verdant pasture where hope is now more potent than our habit of shame. We have been led to a quiet place beside still waters, where we have listened for the reassuring silence. We have learned well the lesson our pain has been sent to teach us, and we intuit that we will return to this place time and again throughout the course of our lives. The shepherd has taught us that without constant prayer, we would be foolish to believe that we might venture forward.

> Yea, though I walk through the valley of the shadow of death,
> I fear no evil: for thou art with me;
> thy rod and thy staff they comfort me.
> *Psalm 23:4*

Finished with the prayer, but only for the moment, we step gingerly upon the path of righteousness where we discover what may well be the most amazing truth yet contained in this psalm. It is this: This life is not about us in the sense that it is not about self-absorption or our many illusions of self-importance. "What?" we are likely to scream in astonishment. "It's not about us? How could that be?" After all, for our entire lives we have been taught that we are the center of everything. We have been conditioned from birth to believe that this life is all about us and, only about us. Our families as well as the culture at large have convinced us that the quality of our lives is quantifiable and is, therefore, about numerous criteria:

- How well we perform

- how much money we make

- how many people we impress

- what we know

- what we do not know

- what credentials we have earned

- how bright we are

- who we know

- what we have

- where we hold our memberships

- what others think about us

- where we grow up

- where we go to school

- what we study

- what grades we earn

- what clubs accept us

- what vocations we choose

- whom we choose to spend our lives with

- how many children we bring into the world

- where they grow up

- where they go to school

- how we vote

- how we invest our dollars

- what we believe to be true

- what we express as our faith

- who our parents are

- what we drive

- what neighborhood we call home

and the list goes on.

At the quiet place by still waters, after a time of being made to lie down we begin to see things much differently. The issues we once believed were important have been turned on their head: and in reality they are of little significance. We have discovered that a big part of what it means to be led into paths of righteousness for the sake of God's holy name is to recognize that we have been mistaken. Our mistake has been an honest one to be sure, but it has been a error nevertheless. We now know that what it means to live this life as the shepherd intends is for us to become the fullest possible expression of love. This is what the psalmist means when he or she informs us that out of our earnest prayers the shepherd shows up to lead us to paths of righteousness for his name's sake. It is clear that the shepherd's mission is to turn us away from our long habit of self-aggrandizement and point us toward a new path where only a faithful few will choose to travel. It is on this road that we will learn to change our thinking from a preoccupation with self to a new commitment to do only the next right thing in the name of the One who first placed our feet upon this path.

One consequence of this shift is that we learn that we may extricate ourselves from life's many equations. This is a liberating discovery. What we find when we are no longer the center of our lives is that the shepherd has taken our place. This perspective is both shaped and buttressed by daily surrender and earnest prayer. Over time we come to realize that doing what is right in the name of the shepherd has become more important to us than concern for our emotional and personal well-being. Our focus upon living life in the name of the shepherd has blessed us with a courage we never knew existed in us.

Strengthened, we are now prepared to approach the valley. But without the perspective born of prayer, it would be unwise for us to take that first step toward the psalmist's image of a valley where we will encounter the shadow of death.

When I was a child, this metaphor terrified me. In my worst nightmares, I imagined the valley as some dangerous locale that had to be avoided at all costs. I prayed my parents would never take me there. As an adult, however, I have come to recognize that the valley of the shadow is not a vacation destination that I can travel through, financing my trip on a credit card. Rather, it is a very real place that exists inside each one of us. Without a doubt its most descriptive name is the one ascribed to it by the psalmist, "the valley of the shadow." This shadowy place cannot be avoided because whether we acknowledge its presence or not, every one of us is at some time in life—usually much sooner than later, required to venture there. We cannot escape this frightening journey because it is our destiny, although the majority of us will do whatever we can to put off the journey for as long as possible. All of us will eventually enter "the valley of the shadow of death."

A word needs to be said here about the emotional power inherent in the word death before we explore this valley. The idea of death immediately evokes fear in every human being. This is because any perceived threat to our survival awakens deep-seated defenses that are fueled by fear. These mechanisms are in place to protect and defend us from all danger and the greatest threat to every human being is, of course, death. Every time we read the word "death," our defense mechanisms kick into action and set us on edge. So it makes sense that as we entertain accepting any invitation to enter a valley named death, we will ponder the dangers and count the potential costs as we feel the tension in us grow.

Blessed with a tension that makes us vigilant, we are now prepared to explore what the psalmist means when he offers this image. The valley is that place where we travel inside ourselves to confront our fears in the holy cause of eliminating anxiety as the driving force in our lives. The journey into the valley is a requisite venture if we hope to become spiritually alive and sensitive human beings. Without a commitment on our part to venture into our shadow, we will never discover our true identities. The tragic consequence of avoiding the valley is that we will fail to learn what it is to surrender our fear-driven lives to the shepherd so that we might come to know what it really means to love. This journey into the shadow, therefore, is essential to every human being who longs to grow spiritually: we cannot make progress unless we are willing to take that first step into this dark and terrifying place.

Interestingly, the poet places this image of the valley immediately following our initial step upon the path of righteousness for his name's sake. Here the psalmist is alluding to the shepherd's truth that once we learn how to walk in the way of right-eousness for the sake of the shepherd's name, there is no turning back. We are irrevocably committed to this path for the remain-der of our lives.

The poet knows that it is necessary for us to stand face-to-face with our fears if we ever hope to find inner peace. Without a willingness on our part to enter the valley, our journey will re-main what it has always been: a painful slogging about in that sticky ooze called denial.

Every human being is called to walk through this valley sim-ply because of the incontrovertible truth of human existence that every one of us will die. The valley, though, is not a me-taphor for our dying, but rather a symbol of what it means for us to accept the reality of our death as the seed of anxiety, that we might learn what it means to have life and to have it abun-dantly. Once we accept the inevitability of our death, we are free to live this existence with a strong sense of the wonderful des-tiny promised to us by the shepherd. It is only through our will-ingness to come face-to-face with our own death, and then to entrust it to the shepherd's care, that we are able to embrace what it means to live with hope for all that lies ahead. Until we are ready to stand face-to-face with death and with every other fear, we will experience no peace, and hope will remain as fleet-ing as a rainbow.

The shepherd knows this: in his commitment to guide us safely toward healing, he recognizes that it is absolutely neces-sary that he lead us into and through the valley of the shadow of death. But before he can lead us, we must first willingly grant him permission to do so.

The shepherd recognizes our reticence. By the millions we human beings try our best to avoid the inevitability of facing our fears and specifically their root, death. In our attempt to escape fear's claim upon us, we are tempted, just as were the children of

Israel who long ago worshipped a golden calf, to bow down to whatever material gods we deceive ourselves into believing will deliver us from death and the anxiety it generates.

In this culture, we make death such a euphemism that it scarcely remains in our consciousness. We glamorize youth and vitality: when death does compel us to pay it some brief attention, we are quick to pay morticians to preserve the remains of our deceased loved ones so that we might view them sleeping in expensive, air-tight caskets where their lifeless bodies are so dressed up and covered in makeup that they appear as if they might stop pretending at any moment, climb out of that box, and dash off to the next party.

At funerals we hug our families, offer time-honored expressions of sympathy, sing beloved hymns, weep in the wake of eulogies, and then depart secretly vowing at some level of our being that in our own lives we won't pause to entertain Hemingway's chilling warning that "the bell tolls for thee." Each of us knows that death's bell will certainly toll for us. But we are determined to ignore that truth for as long as we can put it off and thereby, we believe, delay the arrival of the inevitable. By the vitamins we ingest, by the miles we jog each week, by the makeup we apply and the hair color we use to dye the gray away, we fool ourselves. By the relationships we terminate so that we might seek someone younger and more vivacious, by the alcohol we consume to numb us in our flight from reality, by the goals we set and deceive ourselves into believing are sacrosanct and, therefore, established by heaven, and through our elaborate systems of rationalization, we attempt to avoid the valley by tricking ourselves into believing that we alone may escape death.

But our rendezvous with death and the fear it generates within us cannot be avoided. We may hide from it for years, even for decades, but it can never be escaped. What the psalmist knew long ago, modern psychiatry rediscovered when it made the connection between the stark inevitability of death and humanity's angst.

Whether our fear is viewed through the lens of the psalmist or from the perspective offered by modern science, the results are identical. Anxiety is a given of the human condition and only evolves into a problem (1) when its root is avoided, and (2) when it becomes life's driving force. It is fear that fuels all spiritual illness and all irrational fear flows out of our universal dread of death. Consequently, along with the gift of life comes the obligation to resolve two fundamental questions: (1) Are we willing to accept death as inescapable reality? (2) What responsibility are we willing to assume for living this life the way God intended?

These two questions are so interconnected that for us to strive to make sense and accept the reality of one without doing the same necessary work with the other is akin to a long-distance runner attempting to run a marathon on one leg. It cannot be done.

The psalmist recognizes that death is about life and that life is also about death—the two are so inextricably linked as to be inseparable. This is why the poet structures the psalm with the paths of righteousness immediately preceding the shepherd's call for us to venture into the shadowed valley. What he is explaining is that for us to follow the path of righteousness requires that we trust him to take us to a place where we will be called upon to stand face-to-face with the root of our fears.

The shepherd possesses a secret that no one on this side of the valley can possibly know. Namely, the only safe way out of the valley is for us to enter and walk through it. What the psalmist is teaching is as simple as it is frightening—we must trust the shepherd with our death before we will ever begin to trust him with our life. Left to our own devices, it is quite likely that we will attempt to avoid the valley of the shadow at all costs because, in our long journey on paths of our own construction and in the cause of self-aggrandizement, we have taught ourselves to permit fear to govern our decisions.

Faith invariably requires trust, but the problem here is that trust may only be forged on the anvil of experience. It is because we are afraid that we find ourselves pausing on the path of righteousness, demanding guarantees and warranties prior to our willingness to risk anything. But no such guarantees exist except in our own simple faith in the shepherd. Either we take the risk to trust him and venture forward down the path of righteousness for his name's sake and then into the valley, or we will attempt to avoid both life and the inevitability of death. The tragic result of the latter would be that we will never really live before we are called upon to die. But neither life nor death can be avoided. Those who wait for some kind of warranty settle all too often for the tragedy that a lifetime of fear becomes, languishing in misery until death arrives to end their suffering.

The valley of the shadow of death is the next necessary step on the path of righteousness for his name's sake. It is, therefore, the right path for us. But unless we become willing to enter into its darkness and tremble before fear's long power over our lives, our faith will remain flimsy. It will be nothing more than an anemic allegiance to the doctrines we employ to trick ourselves into believing that we are following God's lead when in truth we are doing nothing more than following our own petty agendas.

The first time I climbed into a raft so that I might float through the Santa Elena Canyon on the Rio Grande, I recall feeling a twinge of anxiety as we drifted deeper and deeper into what was an obviously inhospitable wilderness. After an hour or so had passed, I asked my friend Robert, our guide for the day, what would happen if someone decided to turn back. He smiled, paused, for effect, and said, "There ain't no turning back. Once you get out here, there is only one way out, and that is to go in."

The same is true for this journey into fear. Once we make the decision to trust the shepherd to lead us into the valley, there is no turning back. What is so remarkable about this psalm is how in so few words the poet is able to plumb the depths of the questions that have vexed humanity since our eviction from the primordial garden.

Tomes have been written on what it means for us to negotiate some kind of uneasy peace with death. Yet in this one verse, the poet provides us with a strategy for life that is as simple as it is effective. The psalmist recognizes that courage is not innate to human beings and that it must always be developed as any skill is first learned—and later perfected. The psalmist also teaches us that all real courage is predicated upon trust in the shepherd.

If we are to develop the courage necessary for us to become authentic and faithful human beings, we must learn to trust the shepherd. If we are at all astute, we have learned by now from the pain of being made to lie down in green pastures that we would be wise to never again rely solely on ourselves.

The psalmist tells us that fear has no place in this journey into the shadow, because the shepherd is with us. The word "with" is the operative term here. What it means is not what we think it means at first glance. When someone tells me that they will go with me, whether it is to go fishing or to share a lunch, I understand them to mean that they will join me in some enterprise as an autonomous individual who shares with me necessary boundaries.

However, when the psalmist informs us that he or she does not fear because, in reference to the shepherd, "thou art with me," this means something entirely different from having a friend join us on one of our latest adventures. These words do not in any way suggest a peer relationship. What these four words suggest is that love will protect us from danger, because love is the only force in the whole of the universe more powerful than fear. Because this one who covenants with us to accompany us into the valley is sovereign over everything, even death, fear loses not only its sting, but also its power to convince us to turn back.

Therefore, the shepherd summons us with an invitation that we are free to reject or accept. If we reject it by capitulating to the fear, we will remain on the road to denial. The result is that our living will likely be for the sake of our own self-preservation, as opposed to becoming an existence dedicated to a cause higher than ourselves. Moreover, if we turn back now, we may well live the remainder of our lives under the pretense of being religious, but we will learn little about what it means to trust God. Consequently, peace will elude us. If, however, we accept the invitation, we will enter a valley which is the only place (1) where we will discover the truth about ourselves as we truly are, and (2) where we will, through the process of confronting fear, become cognizant of what it means to trust the shepherd.

Several years ago I wrote a curriculum that merged the "Twelve Steps of Recovery" with responsible Bible study in a small group setting. Immediately upon the publication of this material, I set out to train small group leaders who were then assigned to what I came to call "journey groups." These groups seemed to function well enough for the first three months. Curiously, though, more than half the groups "imploded" by the time they entered midway into the fourth month. At first this phenomenon perplexed me. After interviewing several distraught leaders, many of whom believed they had somehow failed, I began to discern a pattern.

If you have worked the Twelve Steps, you know that Step Four requires that each of us take what is termed a "fearless moral inventory of our own lives." I have often thought that it would be far more accurate to call this inventory a "fearful" moral inventory, because I came to discover that one-half of our groups were falling apart once they entered Step Four.

Why did this happen? Minimal investigation revealed the answer. The participants were afraid to face themselves, and what almost half of them decided to do with their fear was to avoid it. Because of this decision to avoid knowing themselves as they really are, the groups dissolved, and people who might have gained an enormous amount of information about themselves walked away from the experience feeling dejected. I suspect they may have become even more frightened than when they first began their spiritual journey.

In my estimation, the psalmist's valley is synonymous with Step Four. I realize that it is always dangerous to allegorize Scripture, but the psalmist's "valley of the shadow of death" is a cogent and powerful symbol of what it means to be engaged in serious self-investigation.

Most of us are afraid of knowing ourselves as we are. Over and over again, this holds true for people I have counseled and those who have joined me in working the Twelve Steps. I have worked through Step Four so many times that I have lost count. The result of that work is that I know myself better after each time of working the step. Each time I work the step, I have also come to realize that there is always much more to learn about myself.

As people work through the fearless moral inventory, fear looms at every step. No matter how often a person confronts the real self, it never becomes easy.

But remember, all of us are afraid. We are not only afraid of death, the root of all anxiety, but we are also afraid of knowing ourselves and of accepting ourselves as we really are, flaws and all. It is this universal fear of self-awareness that is symbolized in the psalmist's "valley of the shadow of death."

If we refuse to enter this valley, we will have gained very little in the cause of spiritual growth. We may give lip service to surrender and go through the motions of prayer and a righteous stroll in the name of the shepherd, but we will remain hopelessly religious, as opposed to growing toward spiritual maturity. Religious people are invested in their constructed perceptions of God, while spiritual people are dedicated to living in the mysterious experience of God. To be spiritually oriented entails living lives dedicated to the truth that is love. According to the psalmist, the only route to truth is to venture into ourselves. This is always a terrifying proposition.

But the psalmist assures us that as we enter into the shadow, we are to be comforted. Notice, however, that we are not to be comforted by anything of our own making. No, it is only the shepherd's rod and his staff that can nudge us in the direction of courage and hope as we are guided and prodded on a path that we would never dare walk by ourselves.

The shepherd also comforts us with the proclamation that, once in the valley, I will fear no evil. What does this mean? One implication is that this is a solitary journey. No one else can travel with us, just the shepherd. The shepherd is all that we have, and the shepherd is also all that we need. A second implication is that fear is the root of all evil. In the New Testament we are taught that the love of money, as opposed to money itself, that is the root of all evil. But what is the love of money but another name for idolatry? And what generates idolatry but anxiety?

Evil flows out of fear. What the psalmist is teaching us is that once we are in the valley, we have nothing to fear from evil. As soon as we begin to know ourselves as we really are, or become self-conscious, we are not quite so inclined in the direction of evil because our fear about ourselves starts to dissipate. Among other lessons, we learn in the valley is that every human being possesses the potential for evil because all of us are afraid. If sufficient pressure is applied to any of us—even the most spiritually mature—we will be tempted in evil's direction because our fear may rear its ugly head and drive our decisions.

One night when I was in college, a student who was struggling along with me in a particularly rigorous course tapped on the window of my first-floor dormitory room. I raised the window and he immediately climbed in, clutching in his fist a copy of the examination both of us were scheduled to take the next morning. He offered me a glance at the examination questions and, without so much as one twinge of conscience, I grabbed the test and scanned the first question. Once I had finished reading question one, I nodded, signaling that I knew the answer. As my eyes fell upon the first word of the second essay question, I suddenly heard my mother's voice screaming in my head this question: "What in the name of God are you doing?"

I immediately averted my eyes from question two and returned the test to my classmate, who disappeared through the window as silently as he had entered. The next morning as I took the test, I intentionally left question one blank and answered the remainder of the five essays, thus assuring myself no higher a grade than C on the examination.

Had I not succumbed to the temptation to enter into evil, I believe I would have earned an A on that examination. For more than three decades now, I have pondered my readiness to take the first step toward evil because I was afraid. In those days I was terrified of not making good grades, because during the late '60s all of us males who were in college were determined to remain in school and thus avoid the carnage that was Vietnam. But stealing in any form is always evil. Whether it is taking a copy of an examination out of a professor's office or embezzling millions of dollars, it is still evil.

In reading that first question, I was shocked at how willing I was to enter into evil without so much as a thought to the contrary. What the psalmist is telling us, however, is that in the valley we discover that the shepherd's love is a far more potent force than is the fear that drives us to do evil. Through this experience with the shepherd's love and by his gentle guidance we come to understand that evil can flow out of any human heart, no matter how religious. By becoming conscious in the valley of the shadow, we come to discover that frightened part of ourselves where the potential for evil lurks. Because we are aware of this fear within ourselves and also of the reality of the shepherd's sovereignty over evil, the chance of us acting upon fear's summons to do evil diminishes enormously, though never completely.

While I will sin throughout my life, since that moment of my surprising moral lapse more than three decades ago I have never again stolen anything. I remember feeling especially affirmed regarding this issue when I was a seminary student. My Greek professor approached me one morning in the school's printing shop where I worked at the time. He requested that I print on the school's offset press the very final examination that I would be called upon to take the next morning. He handed me the examination in a manila folder and said, "I know you to be a man of character, and I know that I can trust you to print this exam without reading the questions."

I nodded in agreement, but of course I felt like I was drowning in shame as I recalled my secret. The professor abandoned me to the printing of the examination, which I accomplished without reading a word. Years later, when I wrote my very first fearless moral inventory, I described in detail the time in college when I acted upon fear and stole information. What the psalmist is teaching us at this point in the psalm is that the only way out of evil is to become aware of and take ownership of our potential for doing what is not right. This is called consciousness, and it means becoming aware of our strong proclivity for allowing anxiety to have its way with us and also being conscious of God's power to reach even into the core of the most compelling temptations.

In 1999 the United States joined with other NATO forces to bomb Yugoslavia. The goal was to force President Slobodan Malosevic to cease his ruthless campaign of murder and mass deportation of the Muslim Albanians, who have resided for centuries in the province of Kosovo. Most in the west view such murder and mayhem as evil, without a doubt. While Malosevic and his fellow Serbians claim to be Christian, his evil plan is the perverse product of that most heinous unconscious fear that appears all too often as racism.

Whatever else we might choose to say about any human being who would seek to rationalize the evil of genocide under the rubric of ethnic cleansing, we may conclude with confidence that this man has not followed the shepherd into the valley of his own being. Obviously, this man is not conscious, and his evil flows out of his fear in much the same way that raw sewage leaks out of a cracked pipe. Evil is always the same thing—the tragic mark of a living, breathing, but still unconscious human being whose every decision is driven by fear rather than guided by the shepherd's rod and the gentle staff of love.

Human beings who commit evil acts are those who have not ventured into and then out of the valley of the shadow of death. They may well have begun the venture, but they did not complete it because they permitted fear instead of God to serve as their guide. Fear did what it always does: it turned them from the truth—from the truth of God as love and from the truth of their capacity for noble acts and also for heinous crimes.

We do not have to be the president of a sovereign nation to do evil. We all are very capable of doing evil as garden-variety, ordinary, salt-of-the-earth human beings. Evil is not all that complicated. Just as love is the willingness to walk on the path of righteousness surrendered to the shepherd's will, evil begins with the adamant refusal to surrender to anything but our own agendas and to avoid both the shepherd's path and the shepherd's name at all costs. Love is a response to the shepherd's truth, while evil is a reaction to fear's lies.

One of the most interesting men I have met in my twenty-five years of ministry is a professional man who had it all—a lovely wife, two teenage children, a job that paid him more money than he had ever dreamed of, and a home in an exclusive suburb of San Antonio. But one sad day this man's wife requested that he leave their apparently happy home and not return until he could, in her words, "learn to tell the truth." Perplexed and angry, this brilliant gentleman drove one hundred miles north and showed up on the doorstep of my office with a sincere plea for help. We entered into a counseling relationship that continued on a weekly basis for more than three years. In the course of our work together, I learned these four truths about this man: (1) He was, as I suspected, brilliant. (2) His character held the potential for becoming as solid as a block of Texas hill country granite. (3) His view of God was in prodigious need of change. (4) He had yet to make the journey into the valley of the shadow of death because the very idea of any such journey into consciousness terrified him.

During the course of our work, time and again I invited him to join a Twelve Step Recovery group so that he could discover what a terrifying and life-changing privilege it is to travel into that shadow valley that is the locus of fear. In the wake of each invitation, this man regularly found an excuse not to work the Twelve Steps. In his mind, his excuses were solid. After all, in his view he had disciplined himself to tell the truth to his wife, "Things are beginning to work out."

As our work continued, I found myself becoming bogged down by his resistance. He was like many people who come to a counselor's office. He wanted the growth that was necessary to move him through the pain but, like most of us, he was not willing to do what growth requires.

Finally, for a reason that will probably forever remain unclear to me except to describe it as an act of providence, this man entered a Twelve Step Recovery program. Within a few weeks, he willingly and courageously stepped into the psalmist's "valley of the shadow of death" and by his own report he came to discover what he had searched for a lifetime—his authentic self and a God who accepted him just as he is, flaws and all. This man became conscious for the first time in his life. It was out of that consciousness that he came to understand what it truly means to love God, other human beings, and the self in appropriate ways.

Once this man completed Step Four, which is tantamount to stating that he journeyed safely into and out of the valley of the shadow of death, he returned to me for counseling. It was obvious to both of us that we were finished. I recognized it before he did, because I saw in him a radical shift from being fearful and, therefore, reactive in his decisions, to being dedicated to the truth at all costs.

Upon recognizing this major shift in his life, this gifted and good man looked at me and posed this question. "Is this what it means to be born again?"

"Precisely," I responded. "Precisely." Following the insight his question symbolized, we agreed it was time to end the therapy. This man had, with God's help, accomplished what he had come to my office to do. He had willingly and courageously entered into the valley and come out the other side dedicated to the truth, and, therefore, dedicated to God and devoted to all that it can mean for us human beings to love. He had entered the valley awake but unconscious and had come out the other side conscious, able to love his wife and others by telling the truth and by moving, one step at a time, into becoming an authentic expression of the truth.

Today this man is on the path to becoming a spiritual giant. With God's grace he will remain grounded in the truth as he moves toward greater awareness of what it is to love himself and others with an unwavering commitment to veracity.

A strong allegiance to the truth is the fruit of this fearful trek into the valley of the shadow. The psalmist knows this: and furthermore, he or she recognizes that unless we are willing to enter into the valley of the shadow and face our fears, we will never really know the truth, either about ourselves or about God. But for those like the brilliant man who was once so frightened that to save his marriage he once made lying to his wife a habit, the valley of the shadow is the sole place in this existence where we learn (1) the truth about who we really are, flaws, nobility and all, and (2) that God can always be trusted, with our lives, with our most precious dreams, and ultimately with our deaths.

Strengthened by our experience in the valley, we are now prepared for the next step on the road to spiritual maturity, to sit down across the table from our enemies. "May God help us do that," we pray. But what we have learned in the valley of the shadow is that God will help us do exactly that and so much more.

Chapter VI

Thou Preparest a Table

W hen I was too small to help with the farm chores, I would sit in a chair on the edge of my grandmother's kitchen and watch in fascination as she prepared a table for our family. In the piney woods of deep East Texas, the noon meal is called dinner, and because there was still half a day of work to accomplish, that meal was every bit as important as the hearty breakfast we had devoured six hours earlier.

Preparing a table for a family of working folk is no small chore. The linens were lifted that had been draped over the non-perishables since breakfast to keep the pesky flies at bay. Fresh vegetables were steamed, a young rooster was fried, new gravy was stirred into perfection, two pans of hot cornbread—with a sprinkling of sugar added for taste—were baked, and two more pies along with a coconut cake were whipped up. This is what it meant in my childhood for one to prepare a table. It meant to sweat in an unventilated kitchen in the heat of a summer day that was so hot and so laden with humidity that even the cicadas chattering in the chinaberry tree seemed to cry for relief.

Table preparation was hard work requiring a huge measure of love. Within minutes after Grandmother began preparing the table, we would all be seated around it, every one of us named Lively: reverent, hungry, with hands washed clean by cold well water and homemade soap. There we waited for Granddaddy to point to either of his two sons or to one of the grandchildren who might be old enough to respond to his solemn request for a few words of what he called "grace."

> Thou preparest a table before me
> in the presence of mine enemies
>   *Psalm 23:5*

Following a prayer that was usually brief, the family would begin passing plates piled high with every kind of fresh vegetable that fertile acres could produce in those long, hot seasons of my childhood. Once the vegetables were passed, the fried chicken or fried steak or cold slab of smoked ham was offered on platters so heavy that those of us who were not yet old enough to attend school had to be assisted with them.

My brother Bill and I always vied for the wishbone. After dessert, consisting of at least two pieces of pie or one more wedge of sugar-sweetened cornbread dripping in fresh-churned butter and half-drowned in chicken gravy, Bill and I made it our practice to spirit the wishbone away from both the table and adult scrutiny. With the reverence we had learned to express for the sacraments of the old Southern Presbyterian Church, we made a pledge to send our best wish in the direction of the lesser gods who we believed governed such matters as a tug-of-war with a wishbone. Then we each gripped a slippery end of that delicate bone and yanked hard. One end would snap before the other, thus determining the winner. We were certain that whoever won would have his wish granted. I always wished for the same thing—a pony, and though I won half of those contests, no pony ever appeared.

This is what it meant a half-century ago to prepare a table. What was involved when it came to cleaning a table following such a meal was another matter that I avoided, whenever possible, with more than a little cunning.

But in our family, to prepare a table meant to make a prodigious effort in the task of feeding the family so that the adults might be nourished enough to do the work required to keep the farm's meager economy in the black.

While we were far from perfect, we were then and are today a loving family who remain willing to bless each other's uniqueness, to recognize the dignity of every individual, and to forgive the shortcomings of all, no matter what. Even when as a child I regularly spilled my iced tea by placing a full tumbler on a warp in the table constructed by one of my ancestors sometime prior to the Civil War, I would be forgiven. To spill a tumbler full of iced tea guaranteed that a different kind of grace than the words previously offered in the form of a prayer would be demonstrated at this table. To be certain, in the wake of such an always annoying calamity there were the usual grimaces and murmuring of disbelief, but ultimately forgiveness was offered. Mercy was seldom, if ever, spoken. But one of the adults mopped up the mess I had made on the linoleum floor while my grandmother supplied me with a fresh glass of cold tea. Grace at that table was every bit as bountiful as the food.

As a child I found it difficult to appreciate the psalmist's meaning as I pondered the image of someone preparing a table in the presence of mine enemies. In my experience our table was always prepared with love and for the purpose of the family's sustenance. Without my grandparents' trusty refrigerator, the only one they ever purchased, neither the meal nor the leftovers would have been possible. The thing had been manufactured during the earliest days of the Truman administration, and throughout my childhood its reassuring hum became to me a hymn, the very sound of security. When it was running, which it never failed to do, I knew that God was in his heaven, the cows were in the pasture, the hogs were at the trough waiting to be slopped, there was corn to top, cotton to pick, always a better chance than yesterday that the fish would be biting on Silver Creek, and a magnificent table would be prepared for me for the rest of my life.

Everything changes. Today the farm is nothing more than about a hundred and a half acres of nostalgia that invades my soul with such force that I find it uncomfortable to walk through its memories more than once a year. Among the many truths I learned on that red clay—and in the shade of the loblolly pines that I once believed might grow high enough to scrape heaven—was that every time my grandmother prepared a table, her labor was the best expression of love I could imagine.

It would take decades for me to discover what the psalmist probably meant when he wrote: "Thou preparest a table before me in the presence of mine enemies." I think that what he intended is not what I experienced in my grandmother's country kitchen so many years ago.

One morning recently, I was shaving my chin with two or three quick strokes beneath my beard. Though I was in a hurry to get to work to face deadlines that seemed to squawk at me louder than a tree full of magpies, I peered into the tired eyes of the man who stared back at me from the glass.

"You're the enemy," I declared to the face in the mirror, as he offered the same taunt. I wiped the suds from beneath my chin and gave the unexpected exchange little thought until I arrived at my office where, as I sat in my rocking chair, I pondered the meaning of my uncharacteristic outburst in the bathroom only one-half hour before.

I reached for a pad and pen so I might list those I believed to be my enemies. I could think of only one name, and following a moment's worth of head scratching, I struck even that name from the list. My faith in the veracity of Jesus' words had kicked in, and I recognized that as soon as I begin to pray for someone who professes to hate me or who seeks to injure me, that person no longer remains my enemy. I had prayed for the person numerous times; therefore, I could no longer consider this individual to be my enemy.

Perhaps there are those who regard me as their enemy, but they cannot possibly be my enemies unless I first choose to assign them such a designation. Over the course of my life there have been several people who have sought to injure me, who have berated me, slandered me, belittled me, and even on one occasion so skewed the facts as to cause people I regarded as friends to abandon me.

Once I began praying in earnest for good to come into the lives of those who wounded me, I recognized that whatever they did to me was entirely their business and really had nothing to do with me. From this discipline of praying, I also learned that their injurious behavior was probably the product of unconscious projections of their own inner turbulence more than the declaration of any truth about me.

As I returned to the pad with the one written name now crossed out, I decided for the second time that morning that I am my only enemy. My experience is that there are a few people who appear to disapprove of me while a much greater number of people profess to love me. But none of those folks who are displeased with me or who are downright angry with me are my enemy. They cannot become my enemies, as long as I pray for them because status as my enemy is always up to me. I have learned in Recovery that if I am truly powerless anywhere in this life, it is in what other people think of me.

Following my moment in the mirror and the half hour or so alone in my office with my memories and the writing pad, I decided that my problem of having enemies is not an issue that involves other human beings but is always an internal struggle with the parts of me I find difficult to accept.

Soon after this particular moment of anguish, the psalmist's words "Thou preparest a table before me in the presence of mine enemies," assumed a new and unsettling meaning. Just as in those bygone days in my grandmother's kitchen, I now realized that a table, albeit a very different kind of table, had been prepared for me so that I might sit down in the cause of confronting the most difficult challenge anyone might be called upon to experience on the far side of the valley of the shadow of death.

Instead of sitting down with the family that reared me and forgave me often, even when I spilled a tumbler filled with tea, I was now being invited by the shepherd to experience something I was not at all certain I was prepared to face. I suspected that I was on the threshold of learning more than I had ever been willing to know before about what it means to trust, and I now recognized that it would be at this table that I would be called upon to face what I had avoided for a lifetime.

The invitation would require even more trust than I had been willing to muster before I willingly entered the valley. But I had trusted the shepherd to guide me through the shadows, and not one time had this shepherd failed me. Every step of the way on the path of righteousness for his name's sake the shepherd had been there with me comforting me with his rod and with his staff. Now the same path that led me out of the valley had delivered me to this austere table where I would learn another important lesson.

As I approached the table prepared for me by the shepherd, I recognized that I was as ready to do what was required as I would probably ever be. The walk through the valley had bolstered my confidence to the point that I was now willing to trust, for I had come to learn that the shepherd could be trusted even when I was so afraid that I could scarcely stand. My safe passage through the valley strengthened my resolve to complete the journey I had begun. I felt bold enough to heed this latest invitation.

In the heavy silence I fidgeted like a child waiting in the reception room of a dentist's office for that dreaded moment when his name is called. Anxiety hammered my thoughts as though each tentative message of whispered hope was nothing more than a cheap penny nail waiting to be whacked into oblivion. As beads of sweat flowed into the furrows of my brow, I prayed for the strength to trust the one who had guided me through the valley and who now prepared this table for me. Everything in me wanted to run as far as my aching legs would carry me away from this unfamiliar table. But my experience in the valley had taught me to trust a nudge from the shepherd's rod, so I remained seated as I trembled and waited in the menacing silence.

I waited and then I waited some more as I listened to the minute hand on the clock of my imagination ticking evidence of time's crawl toward I knew not what. I wiped the sweat from my brow and stroked my beard as though solace might be found in my whiskers. I considered muttering yet another prayer, as I had done several times before in the valley, but the silence seemed to prefer a reverent anticipation. Again, I returned to the painful enterprise of waiting as acres of hush settled over me like the linens my grandmother long ago laid upon her table to protect its bounty from flies. I listened hard for anything—for signs, for the song of a cardinal, for the scrape of a chair against the floor, for an old man's sneeze in the presence of pepper, for a prayer. Nothing greeted me but eerie silence. The shepherd's rod and staff were no longer visible.

Suddenly a whisper that resembled a breeze hardly strong enough to rattle a branch moaned a word of loathing. This groan informed me that I was weak. Had not that descriptor been the cruel moniker my brother had assigned to me in moments of painful childhood derision? Had he not called me "the weak one?" I choked on the image. I longed to abandon this table. Even the valley was better than this, I imagined. Trust bade me stay. A mental curtain yanked itself open and I stood face-to-face with the ugliness of self-absorption. There I witnessed myself laboring in the soup kitchen in Dallas I had helped to found in the basement of the church. Before me stood a man-child ladling stew to the desperate of Dallas. To my disbelief, I could read my thoughts as they swirled about my head like gnats. What they screamed so shook me that I launched into a defense only to be silenced by the shepherd's silence that bade me listen. The swarm of taunts cried out for my desperate need to be accepted. The man-child knew little except that the accolades he received were never adequate. The truth was that he had no idea what he needed. All he knew was what did not work, but he had never seen fit to swap his quest for praise for anything else.

Next the whisper rattled me like a puppy shakes a sock. This time it spoke of shame. My reflexive reaction was all that I knew to follow. I now pushed hard against the table and turned my face once more in the direction of the valley through which I had safely journeyed. A voice, more soothing than any I had heard since the valley, summoned me to remain at the table. To my surprise, I obeyed. My heart now seemed to lodge itself in my throat, but I obeyed as my knees trembled beneath the table.

"This is too much!" I mumbled through lips as dry as a cotton boll in a drought. Silence ensued and I caught another glimpse of myself in the mirror. "I hate being weak," I cried. Shame broke over me like a wave driven by a hidden storm. "You're dumb!" the voice taunted. "I have done OK!" I argued. "I have figured out how to make it this far in life," I again protested in a less-than-convincing tone. "No, you're dumb. You've fooled people, and the truth is that you're a con man. You're a phony. You're a pseudo-everything. You use a counterfeit faith in God in an attempt to impress people so that they might come to trust you and then love you. You're a phony, Robert Donald Lively. You're a liar. On top of that, you're worthless. You're dangerous because people trust you when they shouldn't. You're never to be trusted. For if people really knew who you were, they'd run away from you as fast as they possibly could. You're a nobody! A nothing!"

The heaviness that now pressed itself against the back of my shoulders was all that held me in the chair. I feared I would suffocate. "Get me out of here!" I shouted to the silence as I struggled to free myself. In the distance I could hear shame taunting me as it slithered away, dragging its vile body over the horizon of consciousness and disappearing into a region I prayed I would never again be required to visit. From the distance I heard its raucous laughter that eventually became muted guffaws.

"I hate this!" I screamed to the silence. The breeze washed against my face, and I dreaded its condemnation.

"No! No! No!" I screamed as loudly as I could. But the breeze refused to heed my protests, and each word I yelled seemed lost immediately in the vacuum that is indifference. Again I yelled as loudly as my lungs could force air through my mouth, but no echo followed. A whisper charged, "You are anger. You are never satisfied. You expect everything when you deserve nothing. You judge harshly. You are very hard on people, often even cruel to others who believe you love them! You're sometimes cruel and terribly unforgiving! You hold fast to grudges because you enjoy them. They supply you with energy. You feed on grudges like hogs gulp slop! Rage sustains you. You relish criticizing. Gossip is your joy; negativity the sum of your faith. You are sin. Not even God could love you! Not even Jesus can save you.

"You may establish all the soup kitchens in the world, but your good works will do nothing to change the truth that you're a hypocrite. You feign love, when in truth your house is built on nothing more substantive than a lifetime of fear. You're afraid of everything—failure as well as success. You can't win. You stutter when you stand before crowds. You lie your way out of all threatening situations. You avoid responsibility and you seek to escape this life, but there is no escape except death and the hell that awaits you. You are a hypocrite; nothing more than an actor. You only went into the ministry to impress others in the hope that someone might love you and think you special. Nobody loves you. Not your family. Not your church. Many in your own denomination regard you as a pariah. That is why you've retreated to a mega-church, so that you can hide while you deceive more gullible people into believing that you're something special, when we both know that you're nothing but a miserable hypocrite."

Thoughts banged together like empty box cars in the night. I yearned to yell, "Shut up!" But I could no longer find the strength. The enemy at this table had proven far too formidable. I could offer no rebuttal.

"You're a conniving con man, Lively. Your sins are not forgiven! If you think you're in hell now, just wait. You ain't seen nothing yet."

That did it. I shut my eyes so tightly that my head suddenly ached as if it were being squeezed in a vise. I more begged than prayed, "God, get me away from this table!" As suddenly as it had begun, the ordeal was over.

Silence returned, this time riding a pine-scented breeze cooled by the snow that lives above the timberline even in summer.

I dared to breathe, lest I suffocate, and a second soothing breeze and then a third washed against my face as I gave consideration to abandoning the table that had been prepared for me. A different voice, this one not my own, admonished me to remain seated. I dared to open my eyes to survey the scene before me—it consisted of nothing more than a bare table, unlike the one prepared for our family by my grandmother.

"What now?" I asked.

Without words, the answer arrived. "Accept."

"Accept what?" I questioned.

"Accept the enemy," Silence whispered.

"I can't do that," I whined.

"It is the only way."

"The only way to what?"

"The only way to what comes next."

"And what is that?" I demanded to know.

"Not until you accept the enemy."

"I can't."

"You must."

"Why?"

"Because the enemy is loved."

"Not by me!" I cried.

"That is correct. But the enemy is loved, nevertheless."

"How could that be?" I screamed with new-found strength.

"Because God loves all of you and accepts all of you."

"But the enemy is a liar," I remonstrated.

"The lies flow out of fear. There is a part of you, in fact, a big part of you that has been afraid all of your life. You will continue to lie until you follow God's lead and accept the reality that you are the enemy."

"But it is still the enemy, even if it is me!"

"And Jesus taught us to pray for our enemies."

"So I am to pray for myself?"

"That is the idea."

"And the enemy will disappear?"

"In time," the voice whispered. "In due time. But first you must trust enough to remain at this table prepared for you so that you might pray that you will accept and embrace with genuine affection and patience the frightened part of you that has lied to you for the whole of your life."

"And if I do not?"

"You can go no further. This is where you, like so many others, will become mired in the irrationality of lies and will live for the remainder of your life with a sense of impending doom."

"So what must I do?"

"Invite the enemy to return to this table prepared for the both of you. Dare to welcome him with genuine sentiments of love. Tell him that you will pray for him and in time that you will come to accept him as the frightened part of you. Once you've done that, pray for him like you've never prayed for anyone or anything before. Pray every waking hour for him. I can't emphasize this enough. Pray and when you're tired of praying for him, pray some more."

"Why?"

"Trust me."

Only because I had traveled safely through the valley and had learned to trust the shepherd, did I accept the invitation. I was shocked to discover what happened next. What occurred was unbelievable, and had even the shepherd told me what this experience was to be like, I would not have believed him—not one word of it. It was that incredible. Even more, it was so wonderful it defies all attempts at description, but I will do my best to describe it, knowing that whatever words I use are inadequate.

Chapter VII

Thou Anointest My Head

All of us fear rejection, and every one of us has experienced it. Rejection is a terrifying issue and one we seem to try to avoid at all costs.

> thou anointest my head with oil;
> my cup runneth over.
> *Psalm 23:5*

I was most fortunate to have been born to a family that did not reject me. Over the past twenty-five years, though, I have worked with many men and women who were in some way, either subtly or dramatically, rejected by their families.

Until I became an adult, I seldom experienced any substantive rejection with the exception of the ordinary tiffs and spats with my peers and siblings. I remember sitting for the SAT with very little anxiety. Today's high school students are required by the combined forces of peer and parental pressure to earn the highest possible score so that they might gain admission to the most prestigious schools. Thirty-five years ago I experienced no external or internal pressure. If others in my peer group felt it, I was not at all aware of it weighing on them and, in retrospect, I suppose that the reason for this disconnection from angst is that it never dawned on me that any college might reject me. When one has no real experience with a certain area of life, there is little awareness.

I took the examination, mailed the scores off to five colleges and universities, and was accepted by all five. I selected my first choice, a small Christian liberal arts college in Sherman, Texas, and relished the idea that I had been accepted one more time.

Once I set foot on that beautiful little campus in the late summer of 1964, I was surprised to discover I was being "sought out." I wasn't at all certain what it meant, but there were young men who seemed to know who I was even before I managed to learn their names. This phenomenon astonished me since it was an experience that did not fit my self-image.

I arrived shy and insecure about almost every area of my life, but I recognized that with effort on my part, I just might make it as a student. What is interesting to me in retrospect is that while I experienced no anxiety regarding being accepted as a student at almost any college, I was not convinced that I was really bright enough to do the work required for graduation from the prestigious little school that accepted me.

Being sought out as one who, with luck, just might be invited to join what was generally regarded as the coolest fraternity on campus was more than I dared hope for. "Why are these guys interested in me?" I asked myself following the first day of new student orientation. "Do they recognize some sterling quality in me that I have missed for the whole of seventeen years of living?" I decided it was more likely that whoever had spread my thin high school reputation one hundred miles or so north must have been gifted in the art of embellishment. If I recognized any truth about myself, it was that I was little more than average as a student, as an athlete, and, for that matter, as a young man. Consequently, I decided that if I had these guys fooled even before I set foot on the campus, then I would permit them to live with the illusion of my special nature for as long as I could, or until the light of truth illumined the shadows of deceit.

After making good enough grades to participate in "rush," I was invited to become a brother of Phi Sigma Something. My relationship with the brotherhood lasted just one miserable semester, during which as a pledge I was physically tortured, humiliated, and ridiculed—all in the perversion of what we were instructed to call brotherly love.

I learned three life lessons from that horrendous experience: (1) I am not a joiner. (2) I detest exclusivity in any form. (3) I had projected a totally false (or inauthentic) image of myself that seemed to attract the attention of what I might best describe as a pseudo-community of young men, most of whom were more gifted than I by every standard of cultural quantification. But these young men were every bit as insecure as I, though neither they nor I would have dared to confess our fears to anyone, not even to ourselves.

I recall the night I received two bids, invitations to join two fraternities. Each student who went through rush was assigned an envelope, and that envelope was dropped into each hopeful participant's campus mail box at a specified time one February evening each year. The envelope might be empty, thus indicating that no invitations were forthcoming—in other words, the student had been rejected by his or her peers.

My fingers went numb as I turned the lock slowly in the direction of its willingness to open the miniature brass door when the numbers were dialed correctly. Through the tiny glass window I could see the long-anticipated envelope resting on its side.

With a hand that now trembled so that I felt embarrassed by my lack of composure, I retrieved the envelope and made a hasty escape to the sidewalk outside the student union building before I decided to pry the thing open. I first raised the sealed envelope slowly in the moonlight and, to my relief, I discovered it was not empty. In winter's dim light I found it impossible to read exactly who had invited me to join their brotherhood, and I had attended the rush parties of two different fraternities. But standing alone on the sidewalk and still trembling—now more from the cold rather than from fear—with the moon as my witness, I sighed.

What I recognized in that moment is that being accepted was all that really mattered. As I ripped open the envelope, I realized, much to my surprise, that both fraternities had invited me to join. At that particular moment the only important thing was that I had been accepted. The two fraternities who invited me into their ranks were as different as a horse is from a mule. One was considered the "brains" fraternity, where the average grade point average, which was a very important index in measuring one's worth on that campus, remained well over three points year after year. The other fraternity was not nearly so academic but was composed of young men who were either on their way to "greatness," in their own vaulted estimations, or were the school's finest athletes, or both.

Giving no thought to the matter, I decided to join the latter fraternity. As I strolled in the direction of where I was told to find my first fraternity party, I happened upon another young man. He rested his bowed frame upon the cold curb and did his best to conceal his sobs. In class only weeks before I had learned the meaning of words I had heard all of my young life about discretion often being the better part of valor. Therefore, I abandoned a man I hardly knew to his misery. It did not require an impressive SAT score to know that, unlike me, this unfortunate student had been rejected. For the rest of my life that image of lonely sorrow would haunt me. In my mind I recorded a warning that read: "Avoid at all costs."

I have come to believe that it is the fear of rejection that drives us to develop an image of ourselves that is not authentic. This inauthentic image, accrued over a lifetime by adding layer upon layer of denial to cover our fear of being found out, is accurately described by the term narcissism.

The fraternity experience served as a mere microcosmic reflection of what I would experience in the adult world. In those college days of long ago we were merely massaging each other's egos, hoping that through being accepted by others, no matter what the cost, we might come to accept ourselves.

The strategy never worked and, in fact, all it did accomplish was the further exacerbation of our raging insecurities. The more we sought to belong, the more we became frightened that we never would. We turned up the volume on our efforts to belong by wearing blue, lightly starched cotton shirts, talking in a code that only we understood, only dating women from acceptable sororities, donning loafers *sans* socks, espousing the same political ideology, and openly shunning anyone with the requisite ego strength to break rank with our allegiance to conformity.

During my freshman year, most of us were not sufficiently well-versed in any of the known disciplines to be wise enough to differentiate a diphthong from a dip stick. Be that as it may, we had already learned an insidious and dangerous message that would take a lifetime to change. That message is contained in this two-word imperative: "Be impressive!"

With that toxic little notion came a constellation of sub-messages, a few of which were these: "Never demonstrate weakness! Always control. Love is sex. Winning is all that matters. Money is God. If you can't take a joke, get lost. Be cool." And of utmost importance, "Make certain that you're 'in,' no matter who you hurt on the way. Be in!"

I assimilated both information in college to regurgitate a sufficient quantity into blue books that I might earn passing marks to qualify me for a degree in four years. But in the perspective offered by thirty years of hindsight, I would have to say that college, more than any other institution, reinforced the culturally sanctioned message of my childhood, "Be impressive!"

Being impressive is the antithesis of being authentic. Of course thirty years ago, even if someone had told me that being authentic was a worthwhile and even essential goal in the cause of developing spiritual maturity, I would not have known what that meant. I had no idea what it meant to be authentic.

All that I knew was what the culture had taught me and what had been reinforced in my four years of college—to be somehow impressive, which is tantamount to commanding me to remain forever dishonest with myself, with God, and with others.

In my life this insidious message produced two results: (1) I learned to do whatever I judged necessary to win favor with those whom I thought might bless me with a dose of acceptance, and (2) for years I hid big chunks of me from myself. I worked to hide what little I knew of the scary and hidden part of me which seemed to appear in the least expected moments with expressions of shame, rage, or criticism directed at others.

In listening to the yearnings of people for the past quarter century as a pastor, I have come to realize that I am not alone in my attempt to hide. Our defense of denial is the primary reason why the shepherd prepares a table for us in the presence of our enemies.

Jesus was right when he commanded us to pray for our enemies, and we ourselves are the enemy. Once we have prayed for those who have hurt us, we have no external enemies. But it is difficult, if not altogether impossible, to offer prayer for ourselves if we do not really know ourselves.

It is only at the table that we are able to learn who we truly are because this is where we bring to the light our goodness as well as those frightened parts of ourselves we erroneously perceive to be reprehensible. Once we have met our enemies, a phenomenon occurs that transcends any effort we might make to comprehend its meaning and to probe its content. We can never understand this phenomenon, because what we experience following our encounter with the enemy is God's mysterious response to our willingness to sit down at the table prepared for us.

In a word, that phenomenon is "acceptance." It is the acceptance of all of us, the good along with the frightened. God accepts the whole package of who we are. This is at least part of what it means when the psalmist assures us that our heads are anointed with oil.

In the ancient culture of the Hebrews, anointing or applying oil to one's body was a sign of a luxury or festivity. When someone experienced great success or there was a celebration, like a wedding, the ancients would anoint themselves with oil.

As a religious rite, anointing became associated with the ritual of consecration. Priests, prophets, and later, kings were anointed by Israel's leaders. The anointing meant that the recipient of this symbol of blessing was regarded as a divine instrument of God's will. The ritual of anointing meant that one had been chosen by God to be of holy service for the remainder of his or her life. Once we have accomplished the hard work of trusting God following our surrender, our journey into fear, and our encounter with the enemy, we recognize, often for the first time in our lives, that we have been accepted all along. In that moment we are transformed from self-absorbed and frightened human beings into people who willingly swap fear for the disciplines required to become the fullest possible expression of God's love.

As we read of this acceptance, our reaction is to disbelieve it, because all of us harbor such unpleasant experiences associated with rejection that it seems impossible that we have been accepted by God. The truth is that we have been accepted from the very beginning, and only fear kept us from knowing it. Now we know that every part of us, especially the parts of us that we have long concealed from ourselves, are accepted. That is the astounding message of the anointing.

I suspect I have as much experience with rejection as with acceptance. I have been rejected for professional positions that I worked hard to win. I have been rejected by people I sought as friends. I have been rejected by the very people I have taught. I have also had people turn their backs on me, hang up on me, turn me down for possible publishing contracts, and refuse me admission to organizations because in their judgment I was not good enough.

Years ago I received a letter from a Presbyterian cathedral in the northeastern United States informing me that, I was not qualified to serve as its pastor. I had not even applied for the position: to this day I have no idea where they happened upon my name. I have not filed a professional resume with the denomination's computer in more than two decades, yet these folks had considered me for the position of senior pastor of one enormous church in a city bigger than any place I have ever visited. I actually felt depressed for not being offered a position for which I had not applied and, until I received the terse letter of rejection, did not even know existed. This is the power of rejection to make us feel crazy.

It is when we rise to leave the table prepared for us, following our courageous encounter with the enemy, that we first feel the oil of divine acceptance dripping from our heads and into our faces. It flows across our brow and rolls down our nose until, one drop at a time, it falls upon our lips where it tastes of a sweetness that surpasses even Tupelo honey.

At first we do not know what to make of this anointing, although if we pause to listen, we discover that its message liberates us from the fear of rejection. In each drop of oil we taste the evidence of the unconditional acceptance of our entire beings, just as we are.

What do we make of this marvelous gift? What response can we offer? How do we live with this truth? Who do we tell? What must we accomplish with this acceptance? What is its cost? How are we now obligated? How will this gift change us?

The psalmist provides us with the answers. He invites us to peer into the cup that the shepherd has placed on the table before us. What is this phenomenon? Before, the cup appeared empty; now it overflows.

The cup is the answer to our every question in the wake of our experience of God's acceptance of us. As we notice the cup, curiosity compels us to pick it up and examine it. Before we can bring the thing close enough for inspection, it surprises us by overflowing.

When the psalmist experienced complete acceptance, the poet recognized the cup as a fitting symbol for the soul. In the wake of God's unconditional acceptance, the psalmist's cup overflowed with joy. This is true for us as well, once we become aware of who we truly are. Moreover, once we experience God's unconditional acceptance of us, flaws and all, our souls cannot contain the joy. Our cup overflows.

The ramifications of this experience are so profound as to defy description. Those of us with long experience in self-loathing experience the end of self-rejection. Further, we come to understand in this anointing that the genuine self-acceptance we received at the table is the solitary path to God. It is only through self-knowledge that we finally come to God so that we might know the power of heaven's acceptance to change us from self-defeating human beings to grateful pilgrims now well along the path that can lead to sainthood. Through self-acceptance at the table and heaven's acceptance, signified by the anointing, we finally learn that our value as human beings has absolutely nothing to do with our so-called triumphs. Nor is our worth linked to the shame we attach to those lessons that for so long we erroneously termed failures.

Before we dared to take that first step upon the path of righteousness that directed us to a valley and to a table prepared for us, we did not know this truth. Perhaps the psalmist was one of the first human beings to learn this important lesson. His experience with the power of the overflowing cup also appears to be expressed in the New Testament in these words dictated by the Apostle Paul to the church at Rome, "If God is for us, who is against us?" (Rom. 8:31).

What we discover as the cup overflows is the same thing we only began to comprehend earlier on our pilgrimage toward the valley. This life is not about us being satisfied and happy: it is only about love. Therefore, whether we experience acceptance or rejection from other people never has to be an issue for us again because, like the psalmist and the apostle, we know that God is for us. We also come to recognize as a certainty that no one can ever really reject us again. We now understand that all of our former experience with rejection in this world has been exclusively temporal and superficial, while God's acceptance of us is both absolute and eternal.

God's acceptance is all that really matters. Once we have sat at the table prepared for us, we discover for the first time in our lives the courage to accept ourselves, even those parts of ourselves we once viewed as shameful and reprehensible. After we have done the courageous work the shepherd requires of us at the table, this world's rejection loses its sting. We know that God accepts us and that what other people think of us—for good or for ill—is of no lasting importance.

Some years ago a bright, articulate, and dedicated young man called me and asked if he might purchase an hour or so of my time. I listened to his request and responded with words that I could tell caused him to pause in what I was certain was bewilderment. I said, "I have discovered that the time I enjoy upon this earth is not my time but belongs to God. Therefore, you can't purchase it. It is free and yes, you can have as much of

God's time as you want. For it is only mine to give away, but it is never mine to sell."

Now obviously confused, the young man continued, "Could I come visit with you next Thursday around noon?"

"C'mon," I said.

On the appointed morning, the young man arrived in the hallway leading to my office carrying a briefcase and wearing a grin that appeared to be painted on by habit more than it was an authentic expression of temperament.

I extended my hand, shook his, invited him into my small, cluttered, but friendly office, and motioned for him to sit. Resting in my favorite rocker, I asked, "What, if anything, can I do for you?"

"I am depressed," the young man spoke, with the painted smile now turning to a definite scowl.

"What are you depressed about?" I inquired.

"Well, I am a minister, and I live in Dallas . . ."

I interrupted, "That is plenty to be depressed about right there."

As I had hoped, the young man chuckled, but I could read the clear signs of sadness in his eyes. With his head bowed and with tears falling to the carpet, I heard him utter words that were not alien to my own experience, but nevertheless they sent chills down my spine.

"I am spiritually ill in that I have lost what little faith I had. All that I am trained to do is to preach and run a church, and I do not even know if I believe in God any more," the man cried.

"I have been there," I assured him.

Glancing up, he asked, "How did you get out?"

I was careful framing my response since I did not wish to add to this young man's pain.

"Well," I said, "let's just say that I have met my enemies at a table prepared for me, and it was in that experience I learned the most important lesson of my life."

"And what was that?" he inquired.

"It is my lesson, so I do not know that I can explain it to you."

"Do you always speak in riddles?" he asked with a hint of frustration in his tone.

I answered, "Far more than I intend to."

"Can you help me?"

"I know two persons who can help you better than I."

"Who?" he asked expectantly.

"Let me ask you some questions."

"I'll do anything to get some relief. Ask me anything."

"Are you sometimes hard on yourself?"

"Yes, very much so," was his sheepish answer.

"Do you fear criticism?"

Again, "Yes."

"Do you feel scared most of the time?"

"All of the time!" was his immediate answer.

"Good," I said, smiling as I realized that this young man so reminded me of myself that I felt it uncomfortable, even painful, to be in his presence.

"Good?" the young minister bellowed. "How could there possibly be any goodness in me living with terror?"

"Because that is what it took to get me to the table."

"What table?" he demanded to know.

"The one prepared for you."

"I do not have a ghost of an idea what you're talking about," he cried in frustration.

"I know," I said as I leaned forward to touch his shoulder with the tips of my fingers.

"I do not know what I am to do," he mumbled between sobs.

"I know. I did not either."

He asked, "How did you find the answer?"

"Well, actually I did not, the Good Shepherd found me."

"Where?" he cried.

"In the core of my pain."

"But what did you do to get out of the pain?"

"I saw that I had to follow the shepherd's lead, and he's one of the two persons who can help you. The other person is you."

Visibly agitated, the young man glared at me and exclaimed, "You realize you're not making any sense. I am hurting so bad, man, I do not know what to do. And someone told me to drive down here to see you, and now all that you do is play with my mind . . ."

"I am not playing with your mind," I said gently. "I know you're scared. I was too, for years, even for decades."

I paused as he gained enough composure to appear ready to listen.

"I invite you to return to Dallas," I said, "and do yourself an enormous favor by finding a good Alcoholics Anonymous group or an Al-Anon group, or some other kind of Twelve Step group. I know that this may sound weird because you're not dealing with an addiction, but I encourage you to work Steps One through Four, because I have found them to be the most efficient spiritual route to the table prepared for you. To be sure, there are countless routes to this table, but the common denominator in all of those paths is pain. And I have come to believe that Steps One through Four are the straightest route into and then out of the pain."

The young man appeared incredulous.

"Alcoholics Anonymous! Man, I don't even drink, and I drove two hundred miles for this? This is insane! I don't need Alcoholics Anonymous! What I need is real help! And I need it now!"

He rose from the chair and said, "I am sorry I wasted your time. For that matter, I am sorry I wasted my time."

With those words, he slipped out of my office quieter than a kitten. There were no amenities offered: no hand shake, no farewell, and no parting shots. Only a silence that now seemed so weighted with gloom that I feared I might suffocate. I suddenly felt consumed with sadness. This gifted young man's pain was kicking up most, if not all, of my issues with myself. Years ago I was exactly where he was that day. It is a place called denial.

I have met many people who, like the young minister, want the pain to stop, but they are terrified to trust. They have learned to trust only themselves with everything. Just as I did years ago, they regularly give eloquent lip service to the God of their frightened faith while they insist upon remaining the shepherd of their own lives.

That is what Moses did until the day a burning bush appeared to him in Jethro's pasture. I suspect it was the disposition of David prior to his encounter with his own sin and with God through the stinging words of the prophet Nathan. As you have read, it was my modus operandi before my discovery of the Twelve Steps of Recovery.

Trust is all that is sufficiently powerful to permit us to step into the valley of the shadow of death. If anything, even more trust is required if we are to sit at the table prepared for us where we will finally come face-to-face with the frightened and denied parts of ourselves.

Hurting people are not likely to discover the truth until they are willing to walk the valley and sit at the table prepared for them. There they will find out that we are accepted! All of us. What is more, we do not have to earn this acceptance. It just happens. It has always been a free gift. But if we are not careful, it is easy for us to miss this wonderful blessing. If we miss the truth that acceptance is always freely given, we will probably spend a good bit of our lives convinced that we can earn it by good works, our eloquent words, a sterling reputation, academic credentials, the praise of our fellow human beings, so-called financial security, and a host of other equally deceptive fantasies.

All that is required for us to experience God's unconditional acceptance is to allow the psalmist's teaching to sink in one day at a time and to trust the shepherd with everything. If we do that, the shepherd will take us exactly where he took the psalmist and every other spiritual giant in the history of faith—to a table prepared for us. There we will discover, to our amazement, that our heads have been anointed with oil as a symbol of heaven's acceptance of our entire beings. Once we embrace this truth, we will see our own cup overflow with more joy than we thought possible.

One recent Easter I was strolling across the huge campus of the church where for the last several years I have served as a visiting teacher and pastoral counselor. For reasons I still cannot fully grasp, that day I was experiencing sadness. This was not depression; it was a rather mild emotional reaction to a small grief that I found myself experiencing regarding the loss of a dream that was dear to me.

During the course of the stroll, I was stopped by perhaps as many as a half dozen members of the church, all of whom were quick to offer me warm Easter greetings. I feigned joy as I nodded to them, but deep inside I was sad.

Alone with my thoughts, I entered the church's cavernous fellowship hall where I saw the cardboard tomb the teachers in the children's department had constructed the week before. I thought I was alone as I approached this miniature tomb, but much to my surprise, one of my little friends, who is two years old, surprised me by jumping out of the tomb. This beautiful child's name is Grace. From behind me in a shadowed corner of the room, I heard the little girl's mother exclaim, "Look, Grace just popped out of the tomb."

For the first time that sad Easter Sunday, I chuckled. I said to my little friend, who comes regularly to my office to receive a sample of the chocolate hearts I keep hidden in a desk drawer, "Thank you, Grace, for showing me the truth of Easter. I was too preoccupied with myself to see."

In this life as well as beyond this life, such is our destiny—to stand as witnesses to the amazing reality that there is not a tomb that has been or can be constructed that may imprison or bind grace. To have experienced this as an absolute certainty is what it means to have our cup overflow. For it is at the table prepared for us that we can experience the mysterious truth of God's unconditional love. Once the oil pours from heaven and drops upon our lips the sweetness of grace, we discover a truth that we never before dared to risk even imagining. In that moment we know beyond a doubt that God has always loved us in a way we have never understood. In spite of everything, regardless of anything, he has always accepted us completely and without qualification, flaws and all, but we could not know this fully until we sat down at the table and did the work the shepherd required of us.

Once we grow accustomed to this anointing, our cup cannot help but overflow, because this news is too wonderful for us. Whether it takes us a day or decades to accept finally heaven's acceptance of us, the day we do, our cup will overflow and never stop.

Chapter VIII

Goodness and Mercy

A sk any thoughtful reader of Psalm 23 to choose two words
in this line they consider most crucial to a solid interpretation, and I suspect they would select "goodness" and "mercy"
every time. While these words grab our attention and, as we shall
see later, powerfully describe God's nature, they are not as important as two other words in this line, "surely" and "follow."

> Surely goodness and mercy shall follow me
> all the days of my life.
> *Psalm 23:6*

With the opening word "surely," what the psalmist offers is a
rare statement of near certainty. Because there is little certainty
in life, this word sticks out like the proverbial sore thumb, and
represents the closest thing to an absolute we get from the
psalmist. Perhaps the psalmist's near certainty results from having consciously chosen the path of righteousness. This path led
the psalmist into and beyond the valley where a table had been
prepared. At the bountiful table this wise poet dared to sit face
to face with enemies, and the reward for such an encounter was
a cup that overflowed. Apparently, through following this arduous discipline, the psalmist has discovered the deep assurance
that goodness and mercy will, indeed, follow in the days ahead.
Whether looking ahead in promise, or back on actual experience, the surety is unshakable.

It may appear that I am suggesting that the psalmist achieved this sense of near certainty. That is exactly what I am suggesting. The thoughtful reader will ask, "How can you insist that God's acceptance is a gift freely given and only a few paragraphs later declare that the psalmist achieved this perspective?"

This apparent riddle is resolved when we perceive that the gift of acceptance is always freely given, but what the psalmist implies is that it is up to each one of us to achieve the sense of near certainty that attends the gift. Put another way, we will not receive the gift of acceptance unless we have first been willing to trust the shepherd to guide our feet to the path of righteousness. Once on that path, we must have faith that he will lead us into and through the valley that delivers us to that place where we are called upon to meet and accept our enemies. The gift is always freely given, but its reception is contingent upon our willingness to receive it. This does not mean that we earn it, because the shepherd's acceptance of us can never be earned. It does suggest that we must, nevertheless, voluntarily collaborate with the shepherd's acceptance of us, and the form such collaboration assumes is trust.

There is irony in the fact that the route that delivers us ultimately to a place of deep trust begins with fear. The shepherd would have us follow the path that leads us to a valley where we walk, one step at a time, through the experience of fear and toward a table where we meet the parts of ourselves we once perceived as unacceptable. On this path we discover that dread necessarily precedes any celebration, and trust becomes the requirements for truth.

Once we have traveled the shepherd's path, we find ourselves strangely willing to embrace this unconditional acceptance of ourselves as the most wonderful gift we have ever received. We never dared to imagine that such a gift was possible for us. Up to this point in our lives, we have never before been willing to accept ourselves or even be open to the possibility that the shepherd, or anyone else, might accept us unconditionally. Such acceptance has certainly not been our experience in this world. We have always viewed ourselves as much too flawed and far too unworthy for it. In the past we have invested enormous energy in hiding from others and, even more so, from ourselves. Our defense has been denial. But now the tricks we have played for far too long are over. At that place where the path through the valley twists and turns until it finally brings us to a table prepared for us, we discover a reward more fulfilling than our highest hopes.

We now stand in the light, and as we draw the first fresh breath born of this healing gift, we realize that, for the first time in our lives, our most basic fear is lifting. It is far from gone, but it is definitely on the decline. Like a fog touched by the dawn's first light, it has begun to disappear. For the whole of our lives, it has hammered hard upon the door of our imaginations, bringing us one worst-case scenario after another. Year after year we have cowered in the dark corners of our souls, hoping against hope that fear would not break down that door and drag us into its fetid lair.

Because we have been willing to trust, the truth has now claimed us, and we now know that nothing about us and about the way we live our lives will ever be the same. Fear will no longer drive us as it has driven our decisions for decades. Like the psalmist, we are now able to proclaim with joy the near certainty contained in the opening word of this line, "surely." We say to ourselves, as well as to those we love, that because we have experienced firsthand the shepherd's full acceptance of us, there is nothing for us to dread.

Many theories maintain that an immature personality is driven by fear. The more I ponder this idea, the more sense it makes. During the supervision I received in my clinical training as a pastoral counselor, my instructors would regularly pose to me this question: "How do you suppose this client is scaring himself or herself?" Sometimes a second question was this: "How is this person lying to himself or to herself?"

Early on in the course of my two years of training, I came to the conclusion that there was no difference between the two questions. If we are scaring ourselves, we are also lying to ourselves.

One of the many useful aphorisms I learned from a grand man, Dr. Kenneth Pepper, was this: "A problem well-stated is half solved." These were the words he often employed in training those of us who were beginning therapists to develop a solid diagnosis before we ever thought about development of a treatment plan.

Over the years since my residency and entering a practice as a pastoral counselor, I have devised many treatment plans for clients whose lives I judged to be driven by fear. Most of those well-conceived plans proved ineffective until the discovery of the amazing power inherent in this psalm for the treatment of what ails most, if not every one of us—and that is fear. It would be a serious diminution of the beauty of this psalm to attempt to truncate its eloquence and power by equating it with some modern how-to theory.

Be that as it may, while Psalm 23 is one of the most eloquent statements of truth ever to inspire the human mind, it is also a very effective treatment plan for fear. But before this divine treatment plan can be helpful to us, we must first establish a solid diagnosis. We must come to admit first that we are immature, at least spiritually, if not otherwise, and second that our lives are now, and have been for years, driven by fear.

The psalmist discovered humanity's single cure for fear, which is to trust the shepherd. As the psalm develops, the thought moves from the tentativeness implied in these words, "Yea, though I walk . . ." to the bold proclamation of the discovered assurance, "Surely goodness and mercy shall follow me all the days of my life." This amazing shift may only be attributed to the psalmist's courageous decision to trust, and in the wake of that decision, to experience to the fullest that which trust requires: a face-to-face encounter with fear.

When we happen upon the word "surely," we might pause to ponder this question: "How often has that word actually meant something?" For most of us, the answer would be seldom. Perhaps when we read this psalm we are so familiar with the words that we blithely skip right over the power inherent in the word "surely."

What the word trumpets is that the psalmist is finished with doubt. Doubt is not in and of itself a bad thing. In fact, it is a necessary part of every individual's spiritual journey. Doubt is the fertile soil of faith. But when faith fails to germinate and spring forth, doubt may then breed the kind of fear that debilitates the human spirit as it nips the buds of hope before truth can flourish.

By employing the word "surely," the psalmist is proclaiming to the ages that not only is doubt conquered, but also that fear has been replaced with trust as life's driving force. What is even more exciting is that the psalmist has bequeathed to each careful reader a step-by-step path out of fear. The word "surely" serves as the exclamation point to that simple, daring plan.

The second most important word I discover in this line is "follow." We are conditioned by the families and the cultural institutions that raise us to be led. As a kid growing up in the '50s, one of the first situation comedies I saw on television was "Father Knows Best." The implication in the title is that human beings are led by other human beings. In this case the family is led by a father who supposedly knows what is best for his wife and three children.

From the time we are able to begin to make sense out of life, we are taught by experience that we are to be led. Even before I entered elementary school, one of my favorite games was known as "Follow the Leader." I remember my mother leading me by the hand to my first class of kindergarten. I recall my teacher taking the leadership role from there. Throughout my academic career, from Mrs. Neeley, my very first teacher, to my professors in seminary, I was led. I was also led by scoutmasters, coaches, peers, pastors, subtle cultural influences, institutional expectations, parents, and by my own conscience.

I even learned to stand in the pew of a Southern Presbyterian church and sing with vigor one of my favorite hymns, "He Leadeth Me." When I was old enough to read, I pored over every detail of the stirring adventure we know today as the Exodus, when Moses led the children of Israel out of bondage and toward their promised destiny.

The result of this lifetime of conditioning is that I learned to embrace as unquestioned fact that much of what it means to live this life responsibly is to allow ourselves to be led. This is a good, even necessary, decision if we ever hope to become socialized.

It is natural for us, then, to equate being led with the assumption that the leader is out in front like Teddy Roosevelt charging up San Juan Hill. But that is not the way the psalmist views the shepherd's way of leadership in the lives of individual believers.

It is obvious that whoever wrote these words knew how to shepherd sheep. I have had no experience as a shepherd, but I did spend part of an afternoon in New Mexico observing a shepherd guide his wayward sheep—with the help of two border collies—toward a stone fold. In that he guided them carefully from the rear, he followed his sheep to safety. If those animals were able to speak, they would, no doubt, describe his guidance from the rear as something very close to "goodness and mercy."

Sure we are sheep in the metaphor, the question that seems to beg for an answer is this: What do we make of the psalmist's implicit claim that we, the only rational creatures on earth, are followed by the leader? The image of a leader following behind those being led contains an amazing insight.

The truth is that in leading us, God seldom appeals to our reason. If God did lead through our gift of reason, the shepherd would a suitable image. This is because our reason, or our rational self, or whatever we choose to term the cognitive/perceptual process of making sense, is the product of our consciousness. Consciousness, by its very nature, reflects what we see: said another way, it is the reality we have become aware of through our senses.

What trails behind us or follows us is, however, not fixed in our awareness unless we pause long enough to turn around and discover its presence and discern its purpose. With amazing eloquence, the psalmist discovers that goodness and mercy will follow for the rest of the days that this human being walks life's path. Through that one word, "follow," we learn a great deal regarding the psalmist's perspective of the place and the unique function of the spirit of God when interacting with the human mind.

If goodness and mercy "follow," then God guides every human being from behind in much the same way a shepherd follows, and thereby directs, a flock of wayward sheep—from the rear. God does not lead through the cognitive/perceptual, or conscious, process of our subjective ordering of reality. The spirit of God works behind the scenes of our perceptions, within our unconscious minds.

The idea of God trailing behind us for the rest of our days with the attributes of goodness and mercy is not some quaint, archaic notion. Rather, it is an astute and amazingly sophisticated insight into how God works to guide us in the cause of changing our minds.

God works by insisting upon remaining hidden, thereby refusing to rob us of our freedom. If God were to step out in front of us and lead us like we were so many soldiers following a field general into the fiery fray, we would cease to possess the gift of free will. No, love requires that we have choice, and God assiduously grants us our freedom through insisting upon leading us most often by following.

How exactly do we interpret the word "follow"? One possible answer to that question is often couched in this aphorism: "One may only view grace in the rearview mirror."

This is a cultural image of God more than it is a biblical perspective. This aphorism points to the simplistic notion that hindsight is always 20/20, while scripture is filled with examples where human beings encountered God person-to-deity. Moses, for example, did not look back over the first decades of his life and then assume that by virtue of signs and signals, Yahweh was summoning him back to Egypt. No, he encountered what was for him a present-tense image of holiness that changed not only the course of his life, but also the history of the world.

Many people have shared with me the blessings that came to them in the guise of personal disasters. Because they have witnessed what their faith informs them is good emerging out of the ashes of disappointment, even tragedy, they have tended to equate their subjective interpretations of experience with the way God works.

My view is that it is indeed possible and much easier for us to see how God has worked in our lives in the past than to make sense out of how God is working out his purpose with us in the present. At the same time, I do not believe that it would be wise to attempt to make of our subjective perspectives any kind of sweeping doctrinal statement of how God works, either in history or in the lives of other human beings.

If this is not what the word "follow" means in the psalm, what does it mean? The psalmist has provided us with the answer to that question by describing God as shepherd. God's goodness and mercy emanate from following quietly behind, rather than from assuming the form of some strutting drum major who bends halfway backwards in a grandiose demonstration of pride before striking up the band.

Curiously, our clue appears to lie with the first word of this line. People who are no longer afraid live this life with an air of unflappable assurance that seems to evade the rest of us. Only because the psalmist has faced fear head-on and, in the process, has learned to trust so completely, does the first word of this line, "surely," carry any weight. The poet is declaring that what before were just possibilities are now givens, as dependable as the seasons and as predictable as dawn's first light.

The two givens are goodness and mercy. Those who are no longer driven and dogged by fear discover that goodness and mercy have become their anchors. Although they, like most of us, were once driven by the demons of fear, they are now sustained *only* by goodness and mercy. In practical terms, what this means is that they, like the psalmist, have walked upon the path of righteousness straight into fear. Through that journey they have discovered a truth that precious few people ever find or can believe—namely, that there is *nothing* to fear.

Where they once invested their energy in fear, dread, worrying, and scurrying about, they now rest in the trusted promise of the shepherd. The demons that breathe down their necks lose all power because goodness and mercy banish the demons of fear. Because of their courage, those who have walked the shepherd's path and sat at the shepherd's table have discovered the truth. That wonderful truth, which is heralded by the fanfare word "surely," is that fear has no more power in their lives.

Their lives are not closer to perfection, and they are no more exempt from pain than when they first decided to trust the shepherd. However, because of their new willingness to trust, their experience in the valley and at the table has forever changed their thinking. Instead of being paralyzed with dread regarding what terrible thing might befall them, they now celebrate every moment—set free by God's grace. They have come to realize that whatever happens, be it wonderful or tragic, the shepherd always follows them with goodness and mercy. Because these two qualities describe accurately the shepherd's nature, those who have walked the path have learned experientially that they can trust the shepherd to discover goodness in even the most terrible tragedy.

Without evidence of such spiritual maturity, all of the above would sound like nothing more than one more preacher's pie-in-the-sky projection of how things ought to be. But there are people who have over the decades lived free from the bondage to fear. In fact, I have witnessed a few of them and have studied them carefully. With each of those individuals, I have walked away convinced that they, like the ancient psalmist, live their lives one day at time, strengthened by the truth that "Surely goodness and mercy shall follow me all the days of my life."

The first who comes to mind is my grandfather. This wonderful man died twenty years ago, and yet I find myself making at least annual pilgrimage to the tiny farmhouse he and my uncle built with their own hands when I was hardly old enough to record memories. Sometimes I wonder, as I drive those pine-wrapped farm-to-market roads deep in East Texas, what keeps bringing me back. Yet every time I amble across the acres that raised and sustained him and his family for more than eight decades, I experience the compelling nature of love. His love attracted me throughout the thirty-two years we shared together upon this planet, and even two decades beyond his passing, I find myself still drawn to the memories of the goodness and mercy this man shared so freely.

When I was five, he took my older brother Bill and me fishing on the slippery banks of Pedro Creek. As I recall, we caught a half dozen bream and perhaps a catfish or two to haul home for my grandmother to fry up with some cornbread and a skillet full of hushpuppies. Once my grandfather announced that it was time for us to pull in our lines, I attempted to beat my brother to the front seat of our '51 Chevrolet so that I could catch more of the evening breeze that seldom found its way into the always stuffy back seat.

Eager to gain the advantage over my brother, I arrived at the car in time to swing open the heavy front door. Before judgment had time to catch up with action, I slammed the thing on the tip of my granddaddy's only glass rod, snapping it into two separate parts. As I gasped, I studied the severed glass rod lying in the grass before my bare toes. I dared not peer into my grandfather's pale blue eyes, yet I could hear him sigh. This was his only rod—his single means of fishing. He was far from a wealthy man. Repairs, I knew, would be as costly to him as purchasing a new rod. I realized that he could not afford either.

To say I felt awful in that moment is to understate the decision that I sealed in my own mind with a gulp. If shame, yelling, and, worse yet, a whipping with a fresh-cut peach switch were to be mine, I recognized I deserved it, and I decided I would suffer my fate with as few tears as possible. I heard my grandfather sigh again as I lifted my gaze only high enough to catch a quick glimpse of my brother bowing his head. I could not decide whether he was staring at the severed rod or praying for me. Once more, my grandfather sighed, and with hands the size of ham hocks and the texture of hen-pecked cobs, he touched my bare shoulder as he whispered, "Son, I wish you hadn't done that. C'mon now, let's go home to supper." And we departed, leaving the severed rod tip to lie for what I suspected would be its own kind of lonely eternity in a clump of soft grass.

That was to be the totality of my punishment. There were no uncontrollable outbursts, no swearing of oaths, no threats, no increase in my chores, and certainly no swings or swats. There were only the heavy sighs, followed by a declaration of the obvious. The three of us then rolled on in the Chevrolet, with me in the front seat, until we arrived at the house where the table Grandmother had prepared awaited our ravenous appetites. As far as I know, my grandfather never shared a word of that incident with my father or even with my grandmother. The pain I caused him remained between the two of us, and he was never mentioned it again.

Some years ago, I traveled alone on those back roads of Houston County, Texas, and I pulled my car over to the side of the two-lane blacktop at a field where some seventy years before, this man cleared an entire pasture with an ax. As I leaned against a fence post, I watched a herd of cows grazing on land that had been a virgin forest before my grandfather arrived, armed only with determination, strength, and a sharp blade. As I admired the cows and listened to some unseen crow bent on mischief, I wondered how it was that my grandfather never once punished any of us, or screamed, or cursed, or lost his composure.

The single idea that carried any merit was that he had learned that there was nothing either in this life or beyond to fear. After surviving the Great Depression and sending his only two sons off to fight fascism, he had made the decision to trust God. Consequently, in his own inimitable way, he had surrendered to the one he called Lord. He had walked the valley and had remained long enough at the table to meet his enemies. From the experience, he became a sincere and humble witness to the truth that fear can be nothing more than a painful choice.

A few weeks before he died from congestive heart disease, the family brought him home to the sleeping porch where we could prop him up so that he might count his cows each evening through the window. One afternoon as the sun was setting, he posed a question to me that I will treasure forever. He asked, "Son, you reckon there's any green pastures up there with the Almighty?"

"I reckon so," I whispered as I gazed longingly into eyes that I knew were filled with more pain than any human being should be called upon to bear.

"I hope so," he mumbled with effort as he raised his tired body slowly so as to brace himself on an elbow. From that position he watched his cows enjoy their peaceful evening in the summer grass.

"I ain't afraid of dying, Bobby," he continued with his eyelids now squeezed tightly shut. "I am just wondering what it will all be like," he concluded before he slumped again into the soft pillow.

Today, I realize that this man who was my grandfather, and who by his own report only went as far in school as algebra, was probably the greatest spiritual teacher I have ever known or will likely meet in this life. I am convinced in retrospect that he achieved that status through his willing collaboration with God to trust so much that fear literally abandoned his consciousness. I do not know how to make the point more strongly than to say that there was no evidence of fear in the man. None!

Still leaning against the fence post and studying the pasture that had once been a forest, I thought of two apt descriptors for my grandfather. They were "goodness" and "mercy." Unwittingly, this man over time became the very character of the One he trusted to guide him through the course of his difficult life, most of which was spent as a sharecropper. With the spiritual discipline that trust requires, he literally became the living evidence of God's power to heal.

Of course as a child I did not begin to understand such things. But since that day so long ago when his disappointment rolled into a sigh punctuated by nothing more threatening than an invitation to join him at the table my beloved grandmother had prepared for us, I have thought about this man. Today, twenty years following his death, I am convinced that he became, through discipline, as much like the shepherd who followed him throughout life as any human being can become goodness and mercy.

I met another such spiritual master quite unexpectedly on a Louisiana bayou not ten miles from the Arkansas line. I had been invited by this man's son to go duck hunting for a couple of days in a nearby swamp. That cold December morning I awakened after what I considered to be an all-too-brief nap, and I trudged from a tiny apartment through the rain toward my host's main house to find my friend and his family preparing breakfast in their kitchen. Because it was raining, I knew that hunting was out of the question.

Disappointed, I poured myself a mug of coffee and retreated to the porch where I sat alone for a few minutes and counted raindrops dripping from the gutter as they fell one by one to the soaked ground below. To my surprise, my friend's father joined me on the porch. For the first few minutes we swapped safe observations, then unexpectedly he launched into the story of his experience with hitting bottom as a result of his long battle with the bottle.

I listened intently. With each detail of this man's life story, I became aware that, like my grandfather, this man, who was not much older than I, had so disciplined himself to trust God that he, too, was no longer afraid. He punctuated each wrenching detail of his alcohol-induced disaster with a protracted sip from his coffee mug. What convinced me that he had become possessed by goodness and mercy were the details of the story of his stay in a treatment center where the roommate assigned to him was a young Black man.

My host for that rain-soaked weekend offered this unsolicited confession: "Prior to my entry into treatment, I was prejudiced against Blacks. But in a few weeks of sharing a room with that man, my Black roommate became my brother."

Hearing that pronouncement, I recognized that fear in this alcoholic's life had been replaced by an authentic love that I could only envy as I sat with him that morning, sipping coffee and watching the slow rain form shallow puddles. It was obvious that this man had walked the valley and met his enemies at the table. Because he had accepted God's anointing, he had become willing to accept a Black man, who until his transformation he had deigned to view not only as the "enemy," but also as the object of a lifetime's worth of disdain.

Fear is the driving force behind bigotry. This man no longer rejected or hated anyone because in the valley and at the table he had learned to accept himself as well as to accept God's anointing as an indescribable blessing. Through the pain of hitting bottom, this man learned what it means to love.

The third such man served as my pastor during the impressionable years of my early childhood. I recall this man sitting in a high-backed chair, telling us stories from the Old Testament so rich in color that the characters Jacob, Esau, Isaac, and Joseph came to life.

For the whole of this man's life, he was a caring pastor serving one mid-sized parish after another. Even today, his mind remains sharp and his character genuinely humble. If this man ever uttered so much as one self-serving sentiment, no one I know ever heard it. He has never sought the limelight for himself, yet in more than a half century of ministry, he has consistently dedicated himself to seeing that others were praised for their hard work and accomplishments.

I attended the memorial service for this man's wife. Not surprisingly, he sought me out for the purpose of thanking me for joining him and his beloved family in worshiping the one who had blessed him with the love of a fine woman for more than half a century. On what had to be the saddest day of his life, this man approached me in a crowded little church in Dallas so that he might shake my hand and offer words of gratitude for my presence.

If I were compelled to limit my description of this man to two words, the choice would be easy. Those words would be "goodness" and "mercy." His character is beyond good, and his life has been, for as long as I have been privileged to know him, the daily demonstration of grace. As with those mentioned above, this humble pastor has disciplined himself for a lifetime to become so absorbed in his creator that his life has become the reflection of the attributes of holiness in the way that a calm mountain lake reflects the snow-capped peaks above. He has collaborated with God to become the image of heaven here on earth, an image unclouded by fear.

The final person who comes to mind is a seemingly ordinary woman who spent her adult life as a wife and mother of two sons. A few years after she married a handsome young soldier home from World War II, she and her new husband purchased the 150 acres that had been on his side of the family for close to a century. And it was on that farm north of Houston that she and her family began an adventure in authentic love that in half a century elevated her to the status of spiritual giant.

Some years ago, her husband died after more than two decades of life as the victim of multiple sclerosis. Until the day this man succumbed to a disease that had left him partially paralyzed and confined to a wheelchair, he greeted everyone he met with the same salutation, whether the ground was covered with ice or the afternoon sun was hot enough to brew tea in a jar. He would begin every conversation with, "It is a good day."

For the years I have known her his wife has lived with the identical spirit of goodness and acceptance. If there is any fear in this widow who continues to run her farm where she tends to the needs of fifty cattle every day of the year, I have never witnessed it.

Like the others mentioned above, she seems to live free from all fear. Her trust is so anchored in the day-to-day reality of God that she lives with a confidence and with an ebullience of spirit that remains virtually free of all negative thoughts and attendant emotions. Over the years her life has become an unspoken expression of gratitude, and whenever I mention her name to anyone in her small Texas town, I am greeted with a knowing smile.

God only knows how many people have been touched, perhaps even healed, by this woman's goodness and grace, but I write without fear of being charged with exaggeration that she ministers to me with love more than anyone I have known since I graduated from seminary twenty-five years ago. Her goodness is palpable without being intrusive or suffocating.

Recently, I was fishing alone on the muddy bank of her tank, which is what a stock pond is called in Texas. Unbeknownst to me she approached my position carrying with her a jug of homemade lemonade. She poured me a glass in silence and returned to her farmhouse two hundred yards from where I sat—hoping that a bass might inconvenience me by taking the plastic lure I had cast upon the ripples.

I rose and watched her slow return up the slight rise that separates the lake from the house. Every step of the way her two faithful dogs, Sam and Bud, trailed behind. On that evening, as the sun slipped behind the stand of tall pine trees that line her yard, I whispered a prayer offering thanksgiving for the beauty of it all. In her mind, those dogs are Sam and Bud, but on that sultry, rose-colored evening, I saw profound meaning in that farm woman hauling a half empty jug of lemonade back to her house with two dogs trailing behind.

In her slow trek across that pasture, I witnessed a glimpse, a brief snapshot, if you will, of the destiny of every human being. All of us are called upon to walk alone, and yet we are trailed by two mysterious forces that follow until we are wise enough and sufficiently confident to permit them to catch up with us and, ultimately, to shape.

The four ordinary people I have mentioned here are spiritual giants because they have learned through real life experience to trust even when confronted with evidence that told them that such trust was foolish. Although these four do not know each other, all of them hold two things in common: (1) All of them would agree, I suspect, that the word "surely," became the description of the reliability of God in their lives, and (2) like the poet, they have discovered that goodness and mercy have so followed them all the days of their lives that these forces have overcome them and have even consumed them. Today they stand as the faithful incarnation of those two powerful words. The great miracle they share is that fear is just a memory.

When these people proclaim the seemingly innocuous word "surely," they know as well as the psalmist the impact its meaning has had and continues to have in their lives. Because they have dared to discover the veracity in the word "surely," through the discipline trust requires, they once lived and today live lives that are remarkably free from worry and fear.

If one were to quiz these people regarding their secret of a seemingly happy life, I believe they would offer, in a variety of words and phrases, an identical message. They would tell us that they have walked the valley straight into the core of their fear, and they have dared to face their enemies at a table prepared for them. From these two experiences they have discovered that they may lean on the word "surely" with full confidence. Much to their surprise, they have literally become their destiny in that they have become good and merciful.

Today they serve as witnesses to the rest of us of how it is that our creator would have every human being live. They are the children of an incredible blessing, which has been freely given and simultaneously achieved through discipline, and they and their kind are this troubled world's very best hope.

Chapter IX

and I Will Dwell in the House

As part of the requirements for ordination in the Presbyterian Church, I once sat for fifteen hours of psychological tests over a two day period. On the first day I answered questions for eight hours, and on the second day I followed the same rigorous regimen for seven hours. The single detail I remember thirty years later concerns an exercise where I was offered a blank sheet of paper and was requested by the psychologist to draw a picture of a house.

After giving some brief thought to the challenge, in my imagination I climbed the sand hill above the farmhouse on my grandparents' farm, and drew a quick sketch of the tiny white house that sheltered our family during some of the happiest moments of my life. Since I possess some artistic ability, I considered the exercise to be respite from the other tests that had drained both my energy and my interest. To this day, I do not know what the test meant or whose house I was supposed to draw to satisfy the psychologist regarding my sanity.

and I will dwell in the house of the Lord for ever.
Psalm 23:6

Within a few minutes I handed the rendering to the psychologist. She returned it to me with this question: "So, whose house is this?"

I replied, "It is our house."

"Whose house?" she pushed.

"Our house," I answered.

"Who lives in that house?"

"We do."

"Why do you insist upon being coy?" she asked.

I said something like, "Ma'am, I am not aware of being coy at all. I am simply answering your question. It is our house. It is where we live. We are a family. That means that we love each other. We work hard, and we take care of each other. And we so safeguard each other's freedom that everyone in this family may leave this house safely and venture out into the world to become who God called us to be."

She expressed her exasperation with a sigh that I imagined to be the result of frustration built up during the two days she spent investigating my psyche.

She dismissed me, I finished the tests, and was later declared fit to pursue ordination. But although I was done with those exercises, I have never forgotten the day I drew that house. I suppose I could have drawn any number of the houses or apartment buildings I had inhabited over my young life. But without lengthy consideration, I drew a house which could not have consisted of more than nine-hundred square feet. In its best season that little dwelling could never have been worth more than ten thousand dollars, even wearing a shiny new coat of paint.

I never did discover what the psychologist expected of my drawing of a house, but I have thought about the sketch I made late that March afternoon in 1970. Over the course of three decades I have decided *that* in drawing that house, I was offering a revealing symbol of my life.

Perhaps I chose to draw the house out of the low self-esteem, the diminished sense of self-worth, that has always been an issue with me. In drawing something so diminutive, remote, and seemingly insignificant, I was in one sense describing my view of myself. I do not know if my theory is true because I am not a psychologist. All that I do know is that I automatically drew a tiny farmhouse that sits a quarter mile off a red-dirt road older than the State of Texas.

In truth, I never actually lived in the house, but in another sense, I have lived in it for the whole of my life. Despite all the times I moved, from Texas to Colorado to Missouri to Arkansas, the house remained where my family built it in the shade of three post oaks and one hackberry at the base of a low sand hill lined in pear trees and sturdy pecans. This house was stationary, while I was seeking my identity as well as God's will for my life in distant places. But I knew without question that I was *always* welcome in the tiny farmhouse. Even if I fell on my face, which I was terrified I might do, I realized that those who inhabited the house would take me, no questions asked.

There are probably many reasons I chose to draw that particular house instead of some other house. But that is the house I drew: in retrospect, I believe that I was drawing a self-disclosing image. In that brief moment I was outside of myself, standing alone on the top of the sand hill, gazing down upon something warm, hospitable, nourishing, remote, and isolated from the rest of the world.

No one has lived in that house since my grandmother died some years ago. Today its windows are boarded and the doors locked. Nevertheless, if I were challenged again to draw a house, any house, it would be the one I would sketch on another blank sheet of paper. I suspect I would again be drawing a symbolic picture of my life, because more often than not I feel lonely and perceive myself as insignificant and often isolated from the rest of the world. This house is still *my* house, because this house is where I experienced the power of love to the fullest.

Neither I nor anyone else will ever actually again live in the house: it would need to be razed and rebuilt before it would be suitable for human habitation, but it is still my house. Possibly, though I certainly do not know this to be true, it also is the house of my three brothers and, perhaps, even the house of my four cousins. It is where all of us were loved with physical nourishment, always blessed by prayer, and encouraged to leave, when it was safe to do so, so that we might pursue the dreams that heaven had granted to us as not only our birthright but also as our obligation.

All of us left safely, because we were encouraged to do just that. But I doubt that any of us ever really left at all, because what we experienced in that humble dwelling was inimitable, because the house was safe, affirming, and filled with grace. There is a part of me that always longs to return to the simple dreams I dared dream on the front porch of that little house as I watched puffy summer clouds roll across a sky toward distant places I could only hope I might someday visit.

Over the decades that followed those broiling summer afternoons, I did come to realize many of my dreams. Throughout my adult life, in my mind as well as in my soul, I carried with me every fragrant memory of that tiny farmhouse. The house remained very much a part of me as I meandered about and grew slowly in the direction of seeking to become the best of what the house symbolized.

People who are supposed to know such things tell me that every time we dream of a house, our unconscious is providing us with a rich symbol for our own life. I can think of no reason to question such a theory. In fact, this idea has greatly shaped my view of what I was up to on that day long ago when in response to a psychologist's request, I drew my grandparents' farmhouse.

I think that in drawing that house, I was providing a picture of how I viewed my life in March of 1970. Some may draw a pillared mansion while others of us may sketch an image of a shotgun shanty. But whatever we draw, I believe that in providing an image of a house, we are disclosing important information about how we view our lives.

The psalmist exemplifies this principle. When this ancient poet provides us with the portrait of destiny in the shape of a house, what is being offered is a masterful portrait of spiritual maturity.

The first thing of note in this closing line of Psalm 23 is that the house envisioned is clearly not in the possession of the psalmist, yet, the words tell us that it is in this house that the poet plans to dwell forever.

Obviously, the poet does not envision spending an eternity in a house to which he or she holds the deed. This symbolic declaration is important because it points to the worship of God as opposed to a life of self-absorption. In the mind of the psalmist, the dwelling place established for all eternity belongs not to the self, but rather to the Lord.

The psalmist demonstrates the strong conviction that nothing in the physical world belongs to us. Everything belongs entirely to the Lord, both in this moment and forever.

We are conditioned by a culture driven by fear to think otherwise, but according to the poet, such is the truth. Cultural belief and practice would deceive us into believing that we actually own our lives, as well as the possessions we purchase so that we might clutter up our physical houses with more and more things. According to the psalmist, however, the house in which we are called to dwell is entirely the Lord's and is never ours to possess.

A professor friend of mine shared with me the following revealing anecdote: As he was leaving an evening of "Shakespeare in the Park," he happened to overhear two elderly women discussing this latest production of *Hamlet*. One woman posed this question to the other. "Do not you just love Shakespeare?" To which her companion answered. "No, not particularly. I think he uses far too many cliches."

Perhaps this woman's disdain falls under the rubric of something to do with familiarity breeding contempt. I believe much the same thing happens to us when we read this psalm. Whether we grew up in the church or experienced nothing more than a glancing blow from organized religion, most of us heard or had this psalm read to us long before we were old enough to decide for ourselves what, if any, relevance these words might have for us.

The consequence of such conditioning is that we will probably skip right over the unsettling image of the Lord holding the deed to eternity's house without pausing to think about the implications of this declaration. If the image of a house is a universal symbol of each human being's perception of his or her life, what we are reading here is a truth the poet has found only on this side of the valley and at a table where enemies are invited to sit down as honored guests. The truth uncovered by the psalmist is that our lives do not belong to us, but only to the one whom the poet calls "the Lord" and "my shepherd."

What might come as a shock to many of us is that our time is not, then, our time. Every minute of it belongs to the Lord. Our existence beyond this material realm is also wholly the Lord's province. Our spouses and our children are not ours. They, too, belong to the Lord. Our personal talents or gifts, whether we are painters or singers, preachers or writers, politicians or master teachers, are never ours because they always belong to the Lord.

This discovery brings us full circle to the first two words of this psalm. If we are to embrace the psalmist's truth, every deci-

sion we make must be surrendered to the one who is the land-
lord of this house in which we have been invited to dwell.

This perspective seems to be the greatest mark of spiritual
maturity that any human being can demonstrate. For, once
more, the surrendered life is that arena where the right thing is
done for the sake of the shepherd's name. It is only because the
psalmist has accomplished the difficult work Psalm 23 requires
that of total surrender presents itself as the final exclamation
point to the 113 words that compose this masterpiece.

In writing this book, I have come to realize that the psalm is
the celebration of the successful outcome of one terribly courageous individual's long striving with God. In that sense, it may
also serve as our proclamation of victory over self-defeat, providing we are willing to accomplish the steps enumerated in the
psalm.

Unlike most of us, the psalmist has dared to walk the talk.
This genius has permitted the shepherd to serve as a guide on a
path called righteousness, where one hundred percent of the
recognition for doing the next right thing is given to the Lord.
This poet has successfully followed a road into the valley where
the ultimate human fear has been encountered and endured.
Following that scary sojourn, the poet happened upon a prepared table where the enemy was met, and even embraced,
with a bold new sense of self-acceptance. Perhaps most difficult of all, the psalmist courageously decided to accept the
shepherd's gift of unconditional acceptance. Consequently, a
major shift in perspective took place where all decisions are
now surrendered to the point that what is good for the kingdom of God is regarded as more important than what might
benefit the self.

Any perspective that seeks the Lord's will over satisfying the
self is so rare that it surprises me whenever I bump into it. I have
yet to discover it in the corporate culture, though I would like to

believe that in some small corner of capitalism it has taken root. Because I have precious little direct experience in the business world, I can offer no more information than to say that I have never witnessed it expressed in any context where the bottom line rules.

I have invested the last three decades of my life in Christian ministry. With few exceptions, I have seldom discovered such a perspective in the church, in the seminary, or in church-related institutions. To the contrary, what I most often find in church organizations is a sea of hurting human beings, the majority of whom approach decisions through the lens of self-interest while they speak the language of piety.

Some years ago I was eating breakfast at a table with a group of fellow ministers in the refectory of the seminary from which I had graduated more than a decade before. Predictably, the conversation remained rigidly focused upon religion and the churches we served. Because I am an introvert by nature, I listened while the rest of the ministers at that table shared everything from subjective insights into complex issues to the kind of squeaky clean jokes that often pass for humor in the subculture of American Protestantism.

As I listened, I felt myself becoming agitated. My thoughts changed suddenly from looking forward to the taste of that first bite of a homemade cinnamon roll to longing to be anywhere else but at that table. I surprised myself by rising from my chair. I mumbled a lie as a feeble excuse to men and women who appeared wholly disinterested in whether I remained. I abandoned my uneaten breakfast and escaped that room with its hospitable fragrances so that I might walk as fast as my feet could carry me away from the feelings that seemed at that moment determined to overwhelm me.

I walked in no particular direction. A few blocks from the seminary, it dawned on me that I was scared. "Why?" I asked myself as I panted. The answer was slow to arrive. After walking several more blocks, the insight finally came to me. I realized that everyone at that table was afraid, and either their fear was exacerbating the chronic low-grade anxiety that always whirls about in my soul, or I was taking on their feelings as my own. The farther I walked, the clearer the message became. I was allowing these people to kick up my fear while I was also stooping to pick up their collective angst like it was a heavy bucket of water I had agreed to tote.

With that recognition, I began to feel better, but my thoughts then turned to what it is about being with men and women in my profession that at times feels so uncomfortable. That specific question became the springboard for years of investigation that included psychotherapy and two years of clinical training in pastoral counseling. I have come to realize that ministers sometimes generate within me uncomfortable feelings because for most of my life I have been terribly ill at ease with myself. Simply put, ministers often remind me of me. Therefore, their issues often rub against my wounds, and today I sometimes permit their issues to nip at the parts of me I desperately attempt to avoid knowing.

I now regard that moment at breakfast as the beginning of what for me became a spiritual pilgrimage toward wholeness. What I also discovered on that journey is that I was right about one thing even before I, in the imagery of the psalmist, ever sat down in the presence of those parts of me which terrified me. In particular we ministers are every bit as frightened as the rest of humanity. The reason, I suppose, is that many of us have been taught to rely on the constructs of religion to bring us to consciousness when, in fact, only God can bring us to a place where fear no longer drives our decisions. Because God can never be wholly defined by our creeds, no matter how sophisticated, ministers, like every other human being, are more than a little tentative when it comes to trusting in any reality other than ourselves. We are more comfortable in houses we construct than in God's house.

One consequence of our fear is that we deceive ourselves into believing that this is our ministry, or our church, or our congregation, or our theology, or our mission, or our whatever, when in truth, everything belongs to God. Everything! Often we give lip service to this notion of God's ownership, but even before the words have departed our lips we slip back into odious patterns of thinking, behaving, and feeling that set us up for burnout, bitterness, or both.

If the psalmist committed this error, he or she did not languish in it for long. As mentioned previously, the concluding line of this psalm tells us that the poet knows that all life belongs wholly to the one called Lord. This knowledge is the hard-earned product of disciplined obedience and of uncommon trust.

Early on, and for whatever reason, the psalmist surrenders, and in the process discovers the nature of the shepherd as—simultaneously and mysteriously—sovereign and intimate. From this recognition the poet seems to have arrived at the truth, that any intense commerce with the shepherd significantly dissipates our natural proclivity for wanting. This awareness comes before the poet is made to lie down in a place of hope and also before a brief side trip to a place where restoration is made possible in silence.

The psalmist then chooses to trust, to be directed toward a path of doing the right thing with the credit for all triumphs attributed to the shepherd. From there the path leads into a shadowed valley where fear—even the terrifying inevitability of death—is faced head-on and embraced. Once out of the dark place, the psalmist dares to accept the invitation to sit at a prepared table where he or she meets every part of the self. Having accepted the whole known self, something occurs that obviously surprises the poet. The shepherd shows up and anoints the psalmist's head with oil, signifying that every part of the self has been accepted all along without reservation or condition. The result of this encounter is a joy that outstrips euphoria. From this experience the writer swaps what was likely a life driven by fear for a new existence nurtured every step by goodness and mercy.

The experience described above has provided the poet with a new perspective that is dramatically demonstrated in a celebration where the Lord is declared to be the sole possessor of the poet's destiny. In proclaiming that the Lord's house is destiny's dwelling place, the psalmist is stating that the will of God will forevermore take precedence over every other allegiance.

Such is authentic surrender. The psalmist is now so remarkably absorbed in God that he or she is willing to believe that destiny and joy are synonymous. Because each decision is now surrendered, love, and not self-interest, becomes the driving force for every action. This ancient writer harbors a secret that I suspect none of the overly educated clergy at that breakfast table knew that morning. That truth, once again, is that everything— our lives, our ministry, our dreams, our plans, our congregations, our best efforts, our worst disasters, and the totality of our selves, flaws and all—belongs wholly to God. Nothing in this existence is ours: therefore, while the shepherd calls every human being to be responsible by walking the path of righteousness, none of us is solely responsible for our lives simply because they do not belong to us and they never have. They are in God's possession from the beginning. If we were to elect to be as wise in our spiritual discipline as was the passionate genius who penned this poem three thousand years ago, fear would cease to drive us and joy would, in time, arrive to overtake us.

At the dawn of this new century and a new millennium, I am deeply troubled by the state of our culture's shared life. I have always been put off by the purveyors of a doom and gloom philosophy, and I have read sufficient history to realize that there are those in every generation who suspect that theirs is the most troubled or will be the last before the advent of some great God-ordained cataclysm that will put an end to everything.

However, I am disturbed when I listen to the fear I have come to believe is ubiquitous. Ministers tell me they are not effective. Business people tell me that they do not make enough money. Lawyers tell me that they are afraid that they might lose a big case. Doctors tell me that they are afraid of being sued. Dentists tell me much the same thing. Husbands tell me that they are fearful that they cannot perform sexually. Wives tell me that they are afraid of growing old. Senior citizens tell me that they are afraid of not remaining independent. Adult children tell me that they are afraid to take responsibility for their aging parents. Adolescents tell me that they are afraid of growing up and becoming adults. Students tell me that they are afraid of failing. Teachers tell me that they are afraid of their students' failing and of the wrath of parents and the school board. Recovering fundamentalists tell me that they are still sometimes afraid of God. People of every age and from all walks of life tell me in a variety of subtle ways that they are terribly afraid of being rejected.

If I were compelled to describe the culture in one word, that word would be fear. For we are all afraid, every one of us. Even when we go to church to worship God and study the Bible, we are afraid. We talk about God often in this culture. We pray. We study God, it seems, so that we can study God some more so that we can sound informed the next time we are called upon to study God. Some of us even teach about God. But whatever we do, whether we are in the church every time the door swings open or we quit believing in God about the same time we gave up our interest in romance novels, individually and collectively we are scared.

But the writer of this psalm accomplished something that precious few have. This person actually discovered that his or her destiny is safe through embracing the spiritual principle that the only way out is in. By following a path of doing the next right thing, this ancient poet committed the whole self to God's present acceptance as well as to God's future promise, and the fruit of the experience is a palpable joy that punctuates 113 of the most eloquent words ever written.

When I first began my study of Psalm 23, I was limited by its familiarity. I was so accustomed to its words, meter, and subtle transitions that I convinced myself that I more or less knew its meaning even before I plumbed its depths. I was wrong. Somewhere midway into this study, as I hammered out one idea after another trying to discover something halfway original and also, perhaps, helpful, I was counseling a man for whom fear is the primary driver for every decision. Listening each week for one hour to how it is that fear controls and dominates his life, then returning to this manuscript, the idea came to me one morning that what this psalm best represents is a spiritual discipline, or, if you will, a divine treatment plan for our anxiety. It is God's way of helping each of us through the day.

After several months of living with the psalmist's masterpiece, I have come away from the experience convinced that what were once mere suppositions on my part have become for me the two following truths: (1) This psalm can be viewed as God's prescription for our pain, and (2) the writer of this psalm discovered the path out of the quagmire that is fear.

In outline form, the path out of our pain looks something like this:

- We surrender and thereby discover that this Lord is both sovereign and mysteriously intimate.

- We experience the unexpected reduction of our tendency to want things and success through intense contact with the shepherd, the source of all abundance.

- We are knocked down, and in the wake of humiliation we learn to trust enough to be led to a quiet place where the long process of restoration begins.

- We willingly begin to follow the shepherd's lead on a path toward doing what is right while trying to give all the credit for everything to the guide.

- We face every scary message we have ever uttered to ourselves, and we stare our own death in the face and embrace its harsh, terrifying reality as an inescapable truth. Here we can learn to accept both life and death as wonderful gifts.

- We sit at a table prepared for us where we encounter every dimension of ourselves from the mature to the frightened. In time, we may put our arms around each disparate part of who we are and bring those parts to ourselves as an act of unconditional acceptance.

- When we receive God's anointing of us with oil, following our acceptance of our authentic selves, we recognize the truth that heaven has always accepted us without reservation or condition. Until we arrived at the table, we did not know this.

- When we embrace heaven's acceptance, we experience joy.

- We discover the paradox that instead of leading us, it has followed us all along in the forms of goodness and mercy.

- We come to understand that everything belongs to God—our history and our destiny—and that fear no longer has to control us. With our acceptance of this recognition, we experience our very first taste of genuine freedom.

I suspect that there are as many responses to these 113 words as there are folks to conjure them up. What I have offered on these pages is the result of my own honest probe of one ancient mind's inspired burst of expression in the cause of guiding humanity out of a life of fear and into the fullest possible demonstration of what it means to trust God completely.

This psalm more means what it says than says what it means. Our great challenge is not to figure out what it says, or even what it means, but rather it is to permit these 113 words to speak to each of us in a way that brings us closer to the promise the psalmist talks about in the immortal words: "and I will dwell in the house of the Lord for ever."

Every time we are wise enough to turn to God for help, we take a step toward the safety, security, and shelter of the Lord's house. Whenever we decide to place our trust in the shepherd to lead us, we are choosing wisdom over a fear that possesses the power to disrupt our lives, shatter our dreams, and destroy our best hopes.

The choice is always ours. The shepherd loves us enough to leave the matter up to us. We can choose fear or we can follow the shepherd's lead and step into our worst fears and discover a whole new way of life. In this way, trust in the shepherd becomes the predicate for our every decision, and a sturdy new faith that in time evaporates the fear is our great reward.

Whether or not we choose to heed the shepherd's invitation to trust is likely the greatest question we are called upon to answer. If we choose to heed it, our lives will remain imperfect, but they will be filled with meaning and eventually with a peace that surpasses our understanding. However, if we decline this invitation and place our trust in ourselves, the outcome may well be tragic.

The shepherd knows this, and this is why he summons every human being to leave the unnecessary burden of fear in the dust and step on the path of an exciting spiritual adventure which always leads us to the same place—home.

This book was written as my sincere expression of concern for the abused children of Travis County, Texas. My prayer regarding this endeavor is that through this effort, innocent children may be helped in the name of Him who once said, "Let the children come to me, and do not hinder them; for to such belongs the kingdom of heaven."